saladmeals

Salads to feed body, soul & friends

Hardie Grant

PUBLISHING

saladmeals

EMILY EZEKIEL

PHOTOGRAPHY BY ISSY CROKER

contents

..

salad essentials

..

pantry staples

When it comes to what I like to keep in my pantry, it's always the same. Keep good-quality canned and jarred tuna and anchovies as these can bulk up any meal and add instant umami flavors. Keep bottles of olive oil and vinegars and invest in high-quality spices like za'atar, sumac, and hot pepper flakes, etc. I always have some legumes, such as garbanzo beans, lima beans, and lentils, as well as rice, pasta, and other grains.

1. oils & vinegars
Keep extra-virgin olive oil, regular olive oil, peanut oil, and red and white wine vinegars.

2. honey & maple syrup
These are very useful for adding sweetness to dressings.

3. mustards
Keep a selection of mustards, such as Dijon and English, to add heat to dressings.

4. nuts & seeds
Keep a selection of different nuts and seeds, such as cashews, walnuts, pumpkin seeds, and sunflower seeds.

5. legumes
Canned and dried garbanzo beans, lima beans, and Puy and green lentils are very handy to bulk out salads.

6. spices
Keep coriander, cumin, paprika, sumac, hot pepper flakes, and za'atar in stock.

7. canned & jarred fish
Store good-quality tuna and anchovies to rustle up a salad meal in a matter of minutes.

8. pasta & other grains
Keep a stock of different pastas, rice, and grains such as orecchiette, jasmine rice, farro, and fregola.

..

tools

Everyone needs their favorite equipment to keep them cooking. If you invest in a good sharp knife and good-quality vegetable peeler you will be set. When it comes to salads it's really worth investing in a salad spinner as there is nothing worse than a soggy leaf. As you get more confident in the kitchen and work your way through the following recipes, invest in the equipment that will make your life that bit easier.

1. salad spinner
A must-have for washing and drying delicate salad greens.

2. peeler
A vegetable peeler makes light work of preparing vegetables and fruit.

3. microplane
A must-have tool for finely grating citrus zest.

4. measuring spoons
Always have a set of measuring spoons to accurately measure small amounts of ingredients.

5. knife
Invest in a good-quality sharp knife to help you prepare food quickly and safely.

6. handheld whisk
Very versatile, whisks can add air into a mixture and blend ingredients together as well as whip heavy cream.

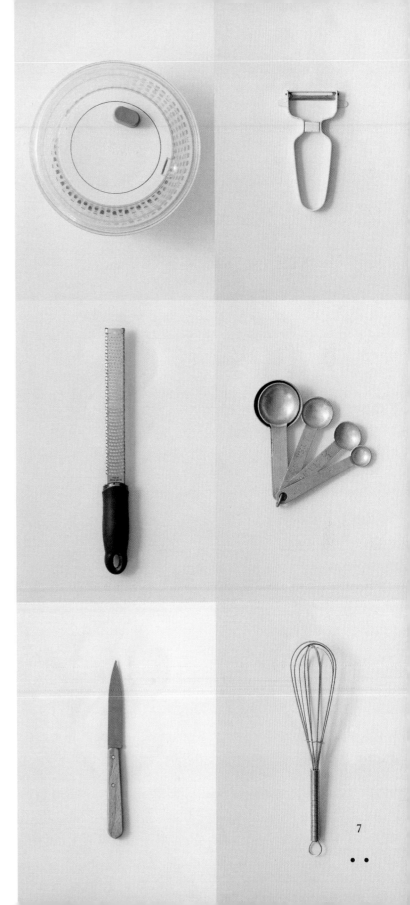

how to

..

wash your vegetables

Many farmers use heavy chemicals and
pesticides when growing and storing
crops, so it's always worth cleaning
vegetables, fruit, and salad before
using. When it comes to fruit and
vegetables, I like to fill the sink with
water, add 1 tablespoon of white wine
vinegar, and let the fruit and vegetables
soak in it for 5 minutes. I then drain
the sink and dry the produce with a
clean cloth or paper towels. Store in
the refrigerator. When it comes to more
delicate salad leaves, tip the leaves into
the basket of a salad spinner and rinse
under cold running water. Spin the
salad dry and store in a Ziplock bag in
the refrigerator until you need it.

..

store your fruit & vegetables

There are a variety of ways to store fruit and vegetables to make sure they keep as fresh as possible. As a basic rule, some vegetables and fruit need to be kept in the refrigerator and others don't. Dark leafy greens, Brussels sprouts, cabbage, salad leaves, herbs, apples, and soft fruit, should all be kept in the refrigerator, while onions, bananas, oranges, and winter squash should be stored on the counter.

1. in plastic
If storing in plastic bags, poke holes in the bag so the vegetable can breathe.

2. in paper
Store mushrooms in paper bags in the refrigerator.

3. in damp paper towels
Use damp paper towels to store herbs, such as cilantro and parsley as well as leafy greens in the refrigerator.

4. in a cold place
Winter squash, pumpkins, onions, and other root vegetables are best stored somewhere cool and dry, such as a cupboard or root cellar.

9

spring

seasonal veggies spring

leaves

lettuce

Lettuce is frequently used as a base for many salad recipes in spring. There are lots of varieties of lettuce to choose from, such as Boston lettuce, Bibb, and watercress, as well as baby salad leaves.

cabbage

Spring cabbages are usually the pointy-headed varieties but spring greens, like collard greens, mustard greens, and turnip greens, are at their best from April until the start of summer.

kale

Kale is available from winter right through to spring. April, May, and June are a good time to find baby kale. There are lots of varieties such as Tuscan kale, Redbor, and curly kale.

chicory

You can eat chicory both as a vegetable and as a salad leaf. As it's quite bitter it pairs well with fruit, such as oranges, as well as peppery radishes. Try the Spring Leafy Salad on page 29.

watercress

Watercress has a slightly bitter, peppery flavor and goes well with many vegetables that we associate with spring, such as fava beans, carrots, and other salad greens.

leaves　　roots

arugula

This spring green has a little bit of a peppery kick to it. It goes well with many other vegetables of spring including fava beans, young peas, pea shoots, asparagus, radishes, and avocado.

spinach

This leafy green goes well in cooling salads and pairs with lots of different foods we associate with spring, such as shrimp, feta, cucumber, and strawberries. Try the Asian Broccoli Salad on page 47.

radishes

Spring radishes are more delicate than winter radishes so they are perfect for using in salads. There are a variety of ways you can use radishes, including lightly roasting them and quick pickling.

new potatoes

New potatoes keep their shape once they are cooked so they can be boiled, fried, or roasted and added to a range of seasonal dishes, such as the Rhubarb & Potato Bake on page 27.

beets

Beets are best from spring until early winter. They have a sweet, earthy taste that goes well with feta, goat cheese, blue cheese, labneh, steamed spring vegetables, radishes, and asparagus.

kitchen garden

Brussels sprouts

Brussels sprouts are usually associated with winter but they are available right through until March. They have a nutty flavor and are great paired with lime, such as on page 29.

purple sprouting broccoli

Purple sprouting broccoli is at its best in spring. It is very versatile and can be eaten on its own as well as working well with fish, such as the salmon on page 47.

cucumber

Baby cucumbers are available this season. Char them or use a vegetable peeler, to make long thin strips to add to salads, such as in the Spring Leafy Salad on page 29.

artichokes

Artichokes have a delicate, sweet flavor and are so versatile—you can broil, grill, steam, braise, or fry them and they go so well with other springtime vegetables.

zucchini

Zucchini with their flowers still attached should be available this season. Try filling the flowers with a delicious cheese stuffing and eating them as part of a platter, as on page 33.

fruit

cherries

Packed with nutrients, cherries are sweet and juicy and go so well with both sweet and savory recipes. They can be added to other spring fruit to make a delicious fruit salad.

rhubarb

Rhubarb has a sharp, tangy flavor and bright pink color. It is at its best from April until June and pairs very well with other foods associated with spring such as strawberries and herbs.

berries

Berries of all kinds are available this season, especially strawberries. Why not pair them with other seasonal fruits and make an elderflower cream, as on page 43.

citrus

All types of citrus, including lemons and oranges, are at their best from winter through to March. They are very versatile and can be added to any dish to lift the flavor.

pomegranate

The sweet-tart flavor of pomegranate seeds packs a huge punch and goes well with other spring fruits and vegetables, such as strawberries, arugula, kale, and citrus fruit.

If you've traveled to Rome in spring, you must have eaten their delicious fried salty artichokes. Pair with a crisp white wine for a spring lunch.

Crispy artichoke salad
with Parmesan dressing

prep time: 30 minutes   **cook time:** 16 minutes   **serves:** 2

• •

juice of 2 lemons

10 baby artichokes

1¼ cups (300ml) light olive oil,
  for deep-frying

3 tablespoons Parmesan Dressing
  (page 186)

1 large handful of arugula leaves

1 head of chicory, leaves separated

1 bunch of chervil

flaky sea salt

½ lemon, cut into wedges, for serving

• •

To prepare the artichokes, fill a large bowl with water and add the lemon juice. Working with one artichoke at a time, trim the stem, snap off the outer leaves until you reach the pale green leaves, then cut off the top third of the artichoke. Halve the artichoke lengthwise and scoop out the fluffy choke. Drop the artichoke into the acidulated water and repeat with the remaining artichokes.

Line a baking sheet with baking parchment. Pour the oil into a medium cast-iron, high-sided skillet, place over medium heat, and heat until it reaches 350°F (180°C) on a thermometer, or carefully drop in a piece of bread and if it turns golden, the oil is ready.

Drain the artichokes and pat them dry on a clean dish towel. Carefully drop half the artichokes into the hot oil and deep-fry for 4 minutes on each side until golden and crisp. Scoop onto the lined baking sheet and repeat with the remaining artichokes. Sprinkle with flaky sea salt and set aside.

Spread the dressing over two plates and top equally with the artichokes, arugula, chicory, and chervil. Serve with lemon wedges.

• •

store/make it vegan
For a vegan option, use the Spicy Herb Dressing (page 186) instead of the Parmesan Dressing.

15

• •

This zesty, sharp, and refreshing
morning salad is always a winner as
it uses the best of the season's citrus
and is topped with pan-fried granola.

rhubarb & citrus salad

with a quick granola topper

prep time: 10 minutes   **cook time:** 10 minutes   **serves:** 2

• •

7 ounces (200g) forced rhubarb,
   sliced into 2-inch (5-cm) chunks

2¾ tablespoons runny honey

zest and juice of 1 lime

½ cup (50g) oats

scant ½ cup (50g) pecans, chopped

⅓ cup (50g) pumpkin seeds

2 tablespoons butter

1 ball of preserved ginger,
   finely chopped

1 large orange

1 blood orange

1 pink grapefruit

1 tablespoon preserved ginger syrup

scant ½ cup (100g) thick
   Greek yogurt

• •

Add the rhubarb to a saucepan with the honey and lime zest and juice. Pour over scant
½ cup (100ml) water and heat over low heat for 5 minutes, or until just soft to the touch.
Remove from the heat and set aside.

Place a large skillet over medium heat, add the oats, pecans, and pumpkin seeds, and
toast for a few minutes, moving the pan around as you go. Add the butter, preserved
ginger, and ginger syrup and toast for 5 minutes, or until golden and crunchy. Transfer
to a bowl and let cool a little.

Peel and cut the oranges and grapefruit into wedges. Spread the yogurt over two plates
and top with a mixture of the citrus fruit. Sprinkle over the rhubarb and finish with the
granola. Eat at once.

• •

store/make it vegan
Make a double batch of the granola topping, then store in a sterilized jar for up two weeks.

• •

This salad brings together the most delicious new potatoes of the season and crunchy, peppery radishes. Serve warm on cooler spring evenings.

roast new potato salad
with feta & roasted radishes

prep time: 5 minutes   **cook time:** 35 minutes   **serves:** 2

• •

7 ounces (200g) mixed radishes

10½ ounces (300g) new
   potatoes, halved

2 tablespoons Citrus Skin Oil
   (page 203) or extra-virgin olive oil

1 red chile, sliced

1 teaspoon fennel seeds

1 lemon, cut into slices

5¼ ounces (150g) feta

1 large handful of watercress

1 handful of toasted whole
   almonds, chopped

½ jar Spicy Herb Dressing
   (page 186)

salt and freshly ground black pepper

• •

Preheat the oven to 400°F (200°C).

Tumble the radishes and potatoes into a large roasting pan with the oil, chile, fennel seeds, and sliced lemon. Toss it all together and season generously with salt and pepper. (Roasting the lemon makes the peel very soft and tender.)

Bake in the oven for 35 minutes, shaking the pan once or twice during roasting. With 15 minutes left to go, crumble the feta over the top, and roast until it is crispy and golden.

Once the potatoes are cooked, remove from the oven, and let cool slightly. Toss the watercress through the potatoes and sprinkle the almonds over the top. Spoon equal amounts of dressing over two plates and top with the salad. Serve at once.

• •

store/make it vegan
You can also make this salad in advance and serve it cold.

19

• •

This salad is a real crowd-pleaser. The crispy croutons cooked underneath the chicken makes them sticky and juicy. Serve warm or cold.

roast chicken salad
with kale & Parmesan dressing

prep time: 10 minutes   **cook time:** 36 minutes   **serves:** 2

• •

4 large chicken thighs, skin-on and
  bone-in

4½ ounces (125g) ciabatta

2 rosemary sprigs

6 garlic cloves, smashed

1 tablespoon fennel seeds

2 tablespoons capers, drained

2 tablespoons olive oil

juice of 1 lemon

1 bunch of kale

2 tablespoons Parmesan Dressing
  (page 186) plus extra for serving

1 head of gem lettuce

1 handful of parsley leaves

1 ounce (30g) Parmesan, shaved

salt and freshly ground black pepper

• •

Preheat the oven to 400°F (200°C).

Place a skillet over medium heat. Season the chicken well with salt and pepper, then place the chicken in the pan, skin-side down, and cook for 5 minutes, or until the skin is golden and crispy. Turn the chicken over and fry for another 5 minutes.

Tear the ciabatta into large pieces, then add them to a roasting pan. Toss in the rosemary, garlic, fennel seeds, and capers. Drizzle over the olive oil and add half of the lemon juice. Toss together. Arrange the chicken, skin-side up, on top of the croutons and roast for 20 minutes. Remove the chicken, toss the croutons, and roast for another 6 minutes, or until golden and crispy.

Remove the inner stem from the kale and shred, add to a large bowl, and squeeze over the remaining lemon juice. Season with salt and give it all a good scrunch. Pour over the dressing and toss well. Separate the lettuce and toss in the leaves with the parsley. Slice the chicken. Divide the leaves between two plates and top with the chicken and croutons. Add the Parmesan and serve with extra dressing.

• •

store/make it vegan

You can also make this salad in advance and serve it cold. Simply dress the salad leaves just before serving.

21

• •

This salad is what dreams are made of—juicy, perfectly cooked steak with crunchy baked fries smothered in a perfect zingy, punchy Dijon dressing.

steak frites salad
with Dijon dressing

prep time: 10 minutes   **cook time:** 25 minutes   **serves:** 2

• •

2 large Maris piper potatoes

4 tablespoons olive oil, plus extra
  for drizzling

3 garlic cloves, sliced

3 rosemary sprigs, leaves shredded

1 tablespoon honey

4 tablespoons white wine vinegar

1 large shallot, finely diced

1 x 9-ounce (250-g) sirloin steak, at
  room temperature

1 little gem lettuce, leaves separated

1 English cucumber, thinly sliced

2 tablespoons Dijon Dressing
  (page 187)

salt and freshly ground black pepper

• •

Preheat the oven to 400°F (200°C).

Using a mandoline, slice the unpeeled potatoes into $\frac{1}{16}$-inch (2-mm) thick fries. Spread the fries out in a single layer on a large baking sheet, toss over the oil, and season with salt. Mix in the garlic and rosemary and bake for 25 minutes, tossing halfway through, until the fries are golden and crisp. Remove from the oven and set aside.

Meanwhile, add the honey and vinegar to a jam jar. Add the shallots, season with salt, close with a lid, and give it a good shake. Set aside.

Place a large skillet over high heat. Drizzle the steak with olive oil and season with salt and pepper. When the pan is searing hot, add the steak, and fry for 3 minutes on each side until golden brown all over. Let the steak rest on a board.

Add the lettuce to a large salad bowl, then add the cucumber and shallots, leaving the vinegar behind. Add the dressing and mix thoroughly until everything is well dressed. Toss in the fries, cut the steak into slices, and arrange on top. Season and serve.

• •

store/make it vegan

Fried celery root steaks or fried smoked tempeh slices work well as a vegan option and be sure to use maple syrup instead of honey.

• •

Roasted, sweet, and earthy beets, partnered with cooling labneh and finished with a herby punch dressing, is a dreamy combination.

roast beet salad
with labneh, soft-boiled eggs & dukkah

prep time: 5 minutes   **cook time:** 40 minutes   **serves:** 2

• •

4 mixed colored beets, such as
   red, orange, and yellow,
   coarsely chopped
zest and juice of 1 lemon
½ bunch of thyme
4 garlic cloves, bashed
1 tablespoon extra-virgin olive oil
2 medium eggs

2 tablespoons store-bought dukkah
scant 1 cup (200g) labneh
2 tablespoons Herby Dressing
   (page 190)
salt and freshly ground black pepper

• •

Preheat the oven to 400°F (200°C). Line a medium baking sheet with a large sheet of foil. The foil needs to be big enough to hold the beets. If the foil is thin double up the sheets. Arrange the beets on the lined baking sheet. Add the lemon zest and juice, then add the thyme, garlic, and olive oil. Season well with salt and pepper, then bring the sides of the foil over the beets and scrunch the top to make a package. Roast for 40 minutes, or until tender, then remove and set aside.

Have a bowl of ice-cold water ready nearby. Bring a small saucepan of water to a boil over medium heat. Gently add the eggs and reduce the heat to a simmer. Cook the eggs for 7 minutes, then add to the ice-cold water.

Tip the dukkah onto a plate. Peel the eggs and roll them in the spice mix. Halve the eggs and sprinkle any remaining dukkah over them.

Spread the labneh over two plates, divide the beets between them, and pour over any extra cooking juices. Top with an egg and drizzle over the dressing.

• •

store/make it vegan
To get ahead, roast the beets in advance, then just boil the eggs and assemble the rest of the salad when you are ready to serve.

• •

Warm roasted new potatoes, sharp,
punchy rhubarb, and creamy
cheddar are a perfect combination
for spring.

rhubarb & potato bake

with watercress & cheddar

prep time: 10 minutes   **cook time:** 30 minutes   **serves:** 2

• •

10½ ounces (300g) new potatoes,
  larger ones halved

3 tablespoons olive oil

1 teaspoon fennel seeds

4 rhubarb stalks, cut into
  2-inch (5-cm) lengths

4 garlic cloves, crushed

2 handfuls of watercress

3½ ounces (100g) cheddar cheese,
  coarsely sliced

1 large handful of fennel flowers and
  fronds or dill

3 tablespoons Dijon Dressing
  (page 187)

• •

Preheat the oven to 400°F (200°C).

Bring the potatoes to a boil in a large saucepan of water, then reduce the heat to a
simmer and cook for 10 minutes, or until the potatoes are tender when stabbed with a
knife. Drain and let steam-dry for 2 minutes.

Add the olive oil, fennel seeds, rhubarb, and crushed garlic to a medium sheet pan and
tip in the potatoes. Toss it all together and roast in the oven for 15 minutes, or until the
rhubarb starts falling apart.

Add the watercress, cheddar, fennel flowers and fronds, and dressing onto the baking
sheet, toss it all together, and serve at once.

• •

store/make it vegan

For a vegan option, omit the cheese and sprinkle over 2 tablespoons nutritional yeast and a
small handful of toasted cashews. Swap the honey in the dressing for maple syrup.

• •

spring leafy salad
with a miso dressing

prep time: 10 minutes   **cook time:** 0 minutes   **serves:** 2

• •

1 head of chicory, leaves separated

1 head of little gem lettuce,
  leaves separated

10 Brussels sprouts

2 red and yellow carrots

2 asparagus spears

1 baby cucumber

3 tablespoons Miso & Lime Dressing
  (page 188)

1 handful of chervil, chopped

1 small bunch of tarragon, chopped

2 tablespoons Pangrattato Crumb
  (page 201)

• •

Place the chicory and lettuce leaves on two individual serving plates.

Finely slice the Brussels sprouts and add to the leaves. Using a vegetable peeler, make long ribbons of the carrots, asparagus, and cucumber. Pour over the dressing, then sprinkle with the herbs and pangrattato crumb. Serve at once.

• •

store/make it vegan
Make a double batch of the dressing and store in the refrigerator for a few days to add to other salads later in the week.

• •

Use whatever new potatoes are in
season, as they'll be fluffy and sweet.
We use the roasting oil as a dressing,
so drizzle any left over at the end.

crispy potatoes
with dates & fresh herbs

prep time: 5 minutes   **cook time:** 40 minutes   **serves:** 2

• •

14 ounces (400g) Pink Fir potatoes
   or new-season baby potatoes

2 tablespoons olive oil

zest and juice of 1 lemon

4 Medjool dates, pitted and chopped

2 tablespoons za'atar

1 tablespoon sumac

1 handful of parsley leaves

1 handful of mint leaves

1 handful of cilantro leaves

2 tablespoons Pickled Onions
   (page 195)

½ cup (50g) grated Comté cheese
   or hard cheese of your choice

salt

• •

Preheat the oven to 400°F (200°C).

Slice the potatoes lengthwise, giving them maximum surface area, then add the
potatoes, cut-side down, to a large baking sheet and drizzle with the olive oil and lemon
juice. Add the chopped dates, season well with salt, and roast for 30 minutes.

After 30 minutes, remove the potatoes and toss in the lemon zest, za'atar, and sumac,
then roast for another 10 minutes, or until the potatoes are golden and crispy in parts.

Toss all the herbs through the potatoes and divide between two plates. Top with the
pickled onions and grated cheese. Eat at once.

• •

store/make it vegan
For a vegan option, just omit the cheese or you can use grated vegan cheese instead.

• •

This salad really sings and is a proper showstopper. It uses the best of what's in season to get the best out of the produce available. Make this platter in any other season—just look for good-quality vegetables, which are crunchy when raw.

sharing platter

spring crudité salad

prep time: 30 minutes   **cook time:** 20 minutes   **serves:** 6

14-ounce (400-g) can garbanzo beans

1 garlic clove, peeled

2 lemons

2 tablespoons tahini

6 tablespoons olive oil

large pinch of hot pepper flakes

14-ounce (400-g) can
   cannellini beans

2 tablespoons za'atar

1 small bunch of heirloom carrots

6 baby cucumbers

6 zucchini with flowers

7 ounces (200g) feta

1 bunch of parsley, chopped

scant ½ cup (100g) Greek yogurt

1 bunch of radishes, thinly sliced

1 head of chicory, leaves separated

3½ ounces (100g) raw peas, halved

1 handful of spring edible flowers

1 tablespoon toasted cumin seeds

1 jar Citrus Dressing (page 190)

salt

1. Preheat the oven to 400°F (200°C). For the hummus, drain and rinse the garbanzo beans, then tip them into a food processor with the garlic.

2. Add the grated lemon zest and juice from one lemon, the tahini, 2 tablespoons of the olive oil, the hot pepper flakes, and a good pinch of salt to the food processor and blitz until it is smooth.

3. Drain the cannellini beans, tip onto a clean dish towel, and pat dry. Spread the beans out onto a large baking sheet and drizzle with the remaining olive oil and the za'atar. Roast for 20 minutes, tossing halfway through, until crispy.

4. Taste the hummus and adjust the seasoning, if needed, then scoop out onto a large platter, spreading it around as you go so all the vegetables have a base to sit on.

5. Using a vegetable peeler, peel strips of carrot and pile onto the hummus. Using a knife, slice the baby cucumbers.

6. Remove the stamens from the zucchini flowers. Whisk the feta, chopped parsley, grated zest from the other lemon, and the yogurt together until smooth. Spoon 1 teaspoon of the mix into the flowers and twist to secure. Add to the platter.

7. Continue to make abundant vegetable piles with the radishes, chicory, and peas. Sprinkle the platter with the crispy cannellini beans.

8. When ready to eat, dress with any edible spring flowers you have, sprinkle over the cumin seeds, and drizzle over the dressing. Serve at once.

Peas and fava beans with creamy burrata is a classic pairing. It's so fresh and delicious and leaves you full of the joys of spring.

fava bean & pea salad
with burrata

prep time: 2 minutes   **cook time:** 5 minutes   **serves:** 2

• •

1¾ cups (200g) podded fava beans

⅔ cup (100g) fresh peas

zest and juice of ½ lemon

3 tablespoons Herby Dressing
   (page190)

1 small handful of mint leaves

1 handful of pea shoots

2 handfuls of mixed leaves

1 handful of Jar Croutons
   (page 200)

2 burratina balls or 1 burrata

salt

• •

Bring a medium saucepan of slightly salted water to a boil over high heat. Add the fava beans and simmer for 4 minutes. Add the peas and cook for another 1 minute. Drain in a colander and briefly rinse under cold running water.

Add the beans and peas to a large bowl, then add the lemon zest and juice, and the dressing, and toss until coated. Add the mint leaves, pea shoots, mixed leaves, and croutons and toss until everything is combined.

Divide the salad between two bowls and place a burratina in the middle of each. If using a burrata, then divide it between the bowls.

• •

store/make it vegan
To make this vegan, leave out the cheese and sprinkle with either roasted cashews or pumpkin seeds.

• •

Crispy garlic mushrooms served with poached eggs is a classic. You can make this throughout the year—just mix up the greens.

mushroom & kale salad

with a poached egg

prep time: 10 minutes   **cook time:** 10 minutes   **serves:** 2

• •

2 shallots, thinly sliced

4 tablespoons white wine vinegar

2 tablespoons butter

1 tablespoon olive oil

14 ounces (400g) mixed
   mushrooms, sliced

3 garlic cloves, sliced

2 eggs

zest and juice of ½ lemon

1 red chile, chopped

1 head of kale, finely shredded

1 large handful of parsley leaves

1 small handful of grated Parmesan

salt

• •

Place the shallots and vinegar in a small bowl, add a good pinch of salt, and set aside.

Place a large skillet over high heat, add the butter, olive oil, and mushrooms and fry for 2 minutes. Add the garlic and fry for another 5 minutes, or until the mushrooms are golden and crisp.

Meanwhile, bring a medium saucepan of water to a boil over high heat. Break the eggs into the boiling water and poach for 3 to 4 minutes until the whites are set and the yolks are still runny. Scoop out the eggs with a slotted spoon and drain on a plate.

Once the mushrooms are cooked, add the lemon zest and chile and remove from the heat. Toss in the kale and parsley, then divide between two bowls. Top with the poached egg, then sprinkle over the shallots and grated Parmesan. Eat at once.

• •

store/make it vegan

You can make the quick pickled shallots in advance and then prepare the rest of the salad when you are ready to eat.

• •

A riff on a classic wedge salad, but we have added a little sweet, smoky vibe. This crunchy salad is a speedy lunch to make in a matter of minutes.

wedge salad
with tahini & lemon dressing

prep time: 5 minutes   **cook time:** 12 minutes   **serves:** 2

• •

⅔ cup (100g) toasted
  buckwheat groats

4 ounces (120g) pancetta, cut
  into dice

½ teaspoon sweet smoked paprika

⅓ cup (50g) smoked almonds, sliced

1 head of iceberg lettuce, chopped
  into wedges

1¾ ounces (50g) blue cheese

4 tablespoons Tahini & Miso
  Dressing (page 187)

salt

1 small handful of chopped chives,
  for garnish

• •

Fill a medium saucepan with water and add the buckwheat. Season with salt and bring to a boil over medium heat. Reduce the heat and simmer for 6 minutes, or until the buckwheat is soft. Drain and set aside.

Dry-fry the pancetta in a medium skillet over medium heat for 6 minutes, or until golden and crisp. Add the cooked buckwheat and fry until the pancetta and buckwheat are golden and crisp. Remove from the heat and toss in the paprika and almonds. Set aside.

Divide the lettuce wedges between two plates and distribute the buckwheat evenly over the top. Crumble over the cheese. Spoon over the pancetta and buckwheat mixture and drizzle over the dressing. Garnish with chives. Serve with any remaining dressing.

• •

store/make it vegan

For a vegan option, omit the pancetta, add 1 tablespoon of oil to the skillet, and toast the almonds and paprika together for a minute, then continue with the rest of the recipe.

• •

Is there anything better than perfectly ripe fruit? If you can't find elderflower cordial, just omit it. Swap the fruit according to the season.

a spring fruit salad

with elderflower cream & toasted hazelnuts

prep time: 5 minutes   **cook time:** 0 minutes   **serves:** 2

• •

scant 1 cup (200ml) heavy cream

1 teaspoon vanilla bean paste

1 tablespoon elderflower cordial

zest and juice of 1 orange

2 apricots, quartered and pitted

1 handful of blackberries, halved

1 handful of strawberries, halved

1 handful of cherries, pitted
 and sliced

⅓ cup (50g) toasted
 hazelnuts, chopped

• •

Using a balloon whisk, whip the cream, vanilla paste, and elderflower cordial together in a medium bowl until you have soft peaks. Add the orange zest and set aside.

Add all the fruit to a large bowl, pour in the orange juice, and toss together.

Scoop the whipped cream mixture onto two plates, making a nest of cream for the fruit to sit in. Add the fruit and sprinkle with the hazelnuts. Serve.

• •

store/make it vegan

To get ahead, whip the cream, vanilla, and elderflower cordial together, then transfer to an airtight container and store in the refrigerator for a few hours before serving.

• •

New-season carrots with their tops are just delicious in spring. Make sure to wash the carrot tops well and coarsely chop them before blending.

spiced carrot salad
with carrot top pesto & crispy garbanzos

prep time: 5 minutes   **cook time:** 20 minutes   **serves:** 2

• •

10 rainbow carrots, with tops

4 tablespoons olive oil

1 teaspoon fennel seeds

1 teaspoon coriander seeds

zest and juice of 1 clementine

1 tablespoon honey

1 handful of smoked almonds

¾ cup (50g) grated Parmesan

1 handful of basil leaves

1 red chile

1 handful of arugula leaves

2 tablespoons Crispy Garbanzo
 Beans (page 198)

salt and freshly ground black pepper

• •

Preheat the oven to 350°F (180°C).

Cut the tops off the carrots and set aside. Halve the large carrots and arrange all of them on a baking sheet. Drizzle over 1 tablespoon of the olive oil, then add the fennel and coriander seeds, clementine zest and juice, and the honey, and mix thoroughly. Season well. Roast for 20 minutes, tossing halfway through.

Meanwhile, add a large handful of the carrot tops to a blender with the almonds, Parmesan, basil, whole chile, the remaining 3 tablespoons olive oil, and 3 tablespoons water. Season with salt and blitz until smooth. Taste and season with extra salt, if needed. Set aside.

Once the carrots are done, remove them from the oven and toss in half the pesto, the arugula, and garbanzo beans. Divide between two plates and serve with an extra drizzle of pesto.

• •

store/make it vegan
For a vegan option, swap the honey for maple syrup and use nutritional yeast instead of the Parmesan in the pesto.

• •

salad in a jar

This is a go-to salad when you feel like some good punchy flavors but want to eat some healthy, nutrient-dense food.

Asian broccoli salad
with hot-smoked salmon

prep time: 10 minutes   **cook time:** 15 minutes   **serves:** 2

1 pound 2 ounces (500g) purple sprouting broccoli

2 tablespoons coconut oil, melted

2 tablespoons tamari

2 tablespoons seasoned rice vinegar

1 tablespoon Sriracha

3 garlic cloves, finely sliced

2-inch (5-cm) piece ginger, sliced

7 ounces (200g) skinless hot-smoked salmon fillet, flaked

2 portions Pickled Onions (page 195)

1 large handful of spinach

1 handful of Umami Toasted Seeds (page 196)

2 tablespoons Peanut & Sesame Dressing (page 191)

Preheat the oven to 480°F (250°C) or as hot as your oven will go.

Cut the large broccoli stems in half, then arrange all the broccoli in a single layer on a large baking sheet. Whisk the melted oil, tamari, vinegar, sriracha, garlic, and ginger together in a small bowl, then pour over the broccoli and toss until combined. Roast for 10 minutes, then turn the broccoli over and roast for another 5 minutes, or until the heads become crispy and sticky. Pile the broccoli into the bottom of two 17-ounce (500-ml) mason jars, add a layer of the salmon, followed by the onions, spinach, and umami seeds. When ready to eat, top with the dressing, close with a lid, and shake well before eating.

store/make it vegan
This is an ideal salad for making in advance and storing in the refrigerator for lunch.

These spiced chops lean heavily on a delicious spice mix called ras el hanout, which is widely available in grocery stores.

spiced lamb chops
& roast eggplant salad

prep time: 5 minutes   **cook time:** 15 minutes   **serves:** 2

• •

2 eggplants, thinly sliced lengthwise

3 tablespoons olive oil

juice of 1 lemon

4 lamb chops

2 tablespoons ras el hanout

1 large handful of parsley, chopped

1 large handful of dill, chopped

⅔ cup (100g) pomegranate seeds

⅓ cup (50g) toasted pine nuts

2 tablespoons Za'atar Dressing
  (page 189)

2 tablespoons pomegranate
  molasses (optional)

salt and freshly ground black pepper

• •

Heat a large stovetop grill pan over high heat. Add the eggplant to a large bowl and drizzle over most of the olive oil. Season generously with salt and pepper, then add to the pan and fry for 2 to 3 minutes on each side until browned. Remove from the pan and squeeze over the lemon juice. Keep the pan on the heat.

Drizzle the lamb chops with the remaining olive oil and sprinkle with the ras el hanout, making sure they are equally coated. Add the chops to the hot pan and grill for 4 minutes on each side.

Toss the parsley, dill, pomegranate seeds, and pine nuts into the eggplant, then divide between two plates. Top with the chops and drizzle over the dressing and pomegranate molasses, if using. Serve at once.

• •

store/make it vegan

For a vegan option, smother a block of firm tofu in the ras el hanout, then cook on a stovetop grill pan until golden on each side. Cut the tofu into pieces and stir through the salad.

• •

A gas cooker flame is used to cook the bell peppers, but you can use a barbecue or broiler instead. If you don't eat anchovies, just omit them.

pepper & bean salad
with anchovies

prep time: 5 minutes   **cook time:** 20 minutes   **serves:** 2

• •

6 red sweet bell peppers

2 garlic cloves, sliced

3½ tablespoons olive oil

1 teaspoon sweet paprika

2 tablespoons sherry wine vinegar

14-ounce (400-g) can
  cannellini beans

6 anchovies in oil

zest of 1 lemon (optional)

1 large bunch of parsley,
  coarsely chopped

salt and freshly ground black pepper

crusty bread, for serving

• •

If you have a gas stove, turn two gas rings onto full flame and drape the peppers over the open flames. Using metal tongs, turn the peppers when they start to go black. You want the whole pepper to be ashy black, so give them time and move them around when needed.

Meanwhile, add the sliced garlic, olive oil, paprika, and vinegar to a large bowl and whisk well with a fork. Season to taste, then set aside.

Transfer the blackened peppers to another bowl, cover with a plate, and let steam and cool for 10 minutes. Once cool enough to handle, slide the charred skin off the peppers and tear the peppers into strips, discarding the seeds and charred skins. Add the peppers to the garlic oil mixture and tip in the cannellini beans, then mix well.

Divide the salad between two bowls, top with the anchovies, grated lemon zest, if using, and parsley. Serve with crusty bread.

• •

store
This is a perfect salad to make in advance and keep in the refrigerator.

• •

This salad is packed with flavor and topped with perfectly cooked duck breasts. Feeling extra hungry? Toss through some cooked rice.

Asian-style duck salad
with kale & Thai chile & ginger dressing

prep time: 10 minutes   **cook time:** 15 minutes   **serves:** 2

• •

1 tablespoon peanut oil

1 head of curly kale, finely shredded

2 duck breasts, about
  12 ounces (340g) total weight

2 small oranges, 1 peeled
  and segmented

1 small red onion, thinly sliced
  into rings

1 chicory, sliced into circles

1 handful of shiso leaves, torn

⅓ cup (50g) Umami Toasted Seeds
  (page 196)

4 tablespoons Thai Chile &
  Ginger Dressing (page 189)

sea salt and freshly ground
  black pepper

• •

Preheat the oven to 425°F (220°C).

Drizzle the peanut oil over the kale and give it all a really good scrunch. Season with salt, then spread out on a large baking sheet and cook in the oven for 10 minutes.

Score the skin of the duck breast at ¾-inch (2-cm) intervals, then season with salt and pepper. Grate over the zest from the whole orange and squeeze over the juice. Place the duck breast, skin-side down, in a cold skillet, then turn the heat onto medium-high. Cook for 8 minutes without moving them or until the skin is golden and crispy.

Meanwhile, toss the kale and roast for another 2 minutes, or until crispy.

Turn the duck over and cook for 4 minutes on the other side, then transfer to a cutting board to rest. Mix the segmented orange, red onion, chicory, shiso, and seeds together in a bowl and drizzle over half the dressing. Mix well and toss through the kale. Slice the duck and arrange on top. Serve with the remaining dressing on the side.

• •

store/make it vegan
For a vegan option, fry some sliced tempeh until golden and crispy, then serve with the salad.

• •

summer

. .

seasonal veggies summer

leaves

lettuce—various

There are lots of different types of lettuce to choose from in the summer, including romaine, butterhead, little gem, iceberg, and looseleaf. Try the Chopped Salad on page 81.

arugula

This summer green goes well with many other foods we associate with summer, such as avocado, cucumber, tomatoes, lemon, basil, and even fruit, such as in the Grilled Fruit Salad on page 71.

spinach

This leafy green goes well in cooling salads and pairs with lots of different foods we associate with summer, such as shrimp, feta, cucumber, and strawberries. Try the Niçoise salad on page 99.

baby watercress

Baby watercress has a fresh, peppery flavor. Sprinkle it over salads or use it as a garnish as in the shrimp cocktail on page 67.

pea shoots & peas

Fresh peas, especially when young, have a mild, sweet flavor and are the epitome of summer. They go well with so many foods including fish, feta, mint, lemon, shallots, and nuts.

roots

kitchen garden

potatoes

Potatoes are very versatile in salads and pair well with lots of different foods that we associate with summer, such as green beans, mustard, olives, red onions, dill pickles, and fresh herbs.

carrots

Bunched carrots are smaller than carrots in the fall and winter. They are tender and very sweet and are great for peeling into long thin ribbons or strips, such as in the Cold Carrot Noodle salad on page 93.

asparagus

Asparagus has a slight earthy, grassy flavor, which goes well with all the foods we associate with summer, such as lemons, tarragon, peas, basil, and spinach.

red onions

Peppery and spicy, red onions in the summer taste a lot sweeter than they do in winter as they haven't been stored for that long. Pair them with tomatoes, cucumbers, and basil. Try the recipe on page 69.

corn

Corn has a sweet, juicy, and nutty flavor and goes so well with lots of different foods that we associate with summer, including leafy greens, potatoes, tomatoes, basil, and shrimp.

kitchen garden

green beans

With their crunchy texture, green beans are perfect to use in salads as they go well with red onions, other beans, tomatoes, cheese, black olives, and eggs.

cucumber

Cucumbers are one of the most popular summer foods. They are cooling and hydrating and are perfect to eat when it's hot as in the Smashed Cucumber Salad on page 83.

tomatoes

Tomatoes are at their best in the summer. They are sweet and flavorful, especially when ripe, and go well with basil, olives, cucumber, feta, Parmesan, avocado, and fennel.

zucchini

Zucchini, whether green or yellow, have a mild, sweet taste. They pair well with many different summer foods, from feta, olives, and eggplant to tomatoes, fennel, carrots, and basil.

avocados

Avocados have a creamy, buttery, and nutty flavor. They match perfectly with other summer foods, such as tomatoes, shrimp, cucumber, olives, and lettuce.

fruit

cherries

Packed with nutrients, cherries are sweet and juicy and go well with both sweet and savory recipes. They can be added to other summer fruit to make a delicious fruit salad.

plums

Available from summer to late fall, plums are sweet, tart, and juicy, depending on the variety. They pair well with other summer fruits, as well as ginger, nuts, yogurt, vanilla, cinnamon, and citrus fruit.

melon

Melon has a floral, fruity, and a sweet flavor, which goes well with other summer foods, such as strawberries, blueberries, mint, cilantro, citrus fruit, and cucumber.

nectarines, peaches & apricots

Juicy, sweet, and tropical, they epitomize summer and pair well with arugula, berries, grapes, lime, mint, tarragon, ginger, cherries, and plums.

summer berries

Strawberries, raspberries, blueberries, and blackberries are all available this season and are extremely versatile. Add them to savory and fruit salads.

Summer is here and this simple
Italian-inspired raw zucchini recipe is
a go-to dish. These zucchini are great
cooked on a barbecue too.

charred zucchini salad
with mozzarella & fregola

prep time: 15 minutes **cook time:** 15 minutes **serves:** 2

• •

generous 1 cup (250g) fregola

zest and juice of 1 lemon

2 tablespoons olive oil

1 tablespoon dried oregano

1 garlic clove, grated

1 red chile, diced

4 mixed zucchini, peeled into
   long thin strips

1 handful of mint leaves

1 handful of basil leaves

1 ball of mozzarella

salt

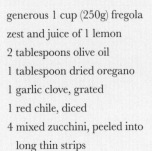

• •

Bring a large saucepan a third of the way up with water to a boil. Season well with salt.
Add the fregola and cook for 10 minutes, then drain and set aside.

Meanwhile, add the lemon juice and zest to a large salad bowl along with the olive oil,
oregano, garlic, and chile.

Heat a stovetop grill pan over high heat. Add the zucchini in a single layer to the hot grill
pan, you may need to do this in batches, and grill for 1 to 2 minutes on each side until
charred and soft. Transfer the zucchini to the oil mix and toss around. Repeat until all
the zucchini is cooked.

Add the fregola to the zucchini, then toss through the herbs and tear in the mozzarella.

• •

store/make it vegan
This salad is great to make in advance and pack up for a picnic.

• •

This salad uses the best of the season's fruit. Make this through the summer as it is a perfect breakfast or dessert for those warm nights.

summer berry salad
tossed with maple, lemon & vanilla

prep time: 10 minutes **cook time:** 0 minutes **serves:** 2

• •

1 handful of raspberries

1 handful of strawberries, chopped

1 handful of cherries, pitted
and halved

zest and juice of ½ lemon

2 tablespoons maple syrup

scant 1 cup (200g) thick
Greek yogurt

1 teaspoon vanilla bean paste

basil leaves, for decoration

• •

Add all the fruit to a large bowl, then add the lemon zest, and squeeze the juice over all the fruit. Drizzle with the maple syrup, mix well, then let marinate for a few minutes.

Mix the yogurt and vanilla together in a bowl until well combined.

Spoon the yogurt into two bowls, top with the fruit, and drizzle over any juices left. Decorate with basil and serve.

• •

store/make it vegan
For a vegan option, swap the Greek yogurt for a vegan soy or coconut yogurt.

• •

Fresh corn sums up summer. Three jalapeño chiles are used here, but if you like a little less heat, then leave one or two out.

corn & orecchiette salad

with cherry tomatoes & ricotta

prep time: 10 minutes   **cook time:** 15 minutes   **serves:** 2

• •

9 ounces (250g) orecchiette

2 tablespoons olive oil

3 garlic cloves, sliced

3 jalapeño chiles, sliced

2 handfuls of mixed cherry
   tomatoes, halved

3 fresh corn on the cobs,
   corn kernels sliced off

scant ½ cup (100g) ricotta

zest and juice of ½ lemon

1 bunch of basil, leaves picked

1 large handful of cilantro,
   leaves picked

salt and freshly ground black pepper

grated Pecorino Romano, for
   serving (optional)

• •

Bring a medium saucepan of well-salted water to a boil over high heat. Add the pasta and cook according to the package directions, about 8 to 10 minutes, until al dente.

Meanwhile, heat the olive oil in a large skillet over medium heat, add the garlic, and fry for 1 minute, or until lightly golden. Add the sliced jalapeños, cherry tomatoes, and corn and cook for 10 minutes.

Once the pasta is cooked, set aside 1 to 1¼ cups (250–300ml) of the cooking water, then drain. Add the pasta to the skillet with the ricotta, the lemon zest and juice, and a splash of the reserved cooking water. Toss, adding a little more cooking water if needed.

Toss through all the herbs and season well to taste. Spoon the pasta into bowls and serve with grated pecorino, if desired.

• •

store/make it vegan
If you want to get ahead, this salad will happily sit in the refrigerator.

• •

This is a super-quick, fresh, and crunchy salad. You can mix in any raw vegetable you desire so it is also very versatile.

green shaved salad
with green goddess jalapeño dressing

prep time: 10 minutes   **cook time:** 6 minutes   **serves:** 2

• •

2 large handful of fresh peas,
   still in their pods

6 asparagus spears

1 head of fennel

1 handful of snow peas, halved

2 tablespoons Green Goddess
   Jalapeño Dressing (page 188)

1 handful of parsley leaves

1 handful of tarragon leaves

1 handful of chopped almonds

• •

Heat a large skillet over high heat. Once hot, add the peas and toast for 6 minutes, or until charred on each side.

Using a vegetable peeler, shave long, thin strips of the asparagus into a large bowl. Halve and quarter the fennel and finely slice.

Toss the peas into the bowl with the snow peas, then divide the salad between two plates, drizzle with the dressing and sprinkle with the herbs and chopped nuts.

• •

store/make it vegan
Make a double batch of the dressing and store in the refrigerator for a few days to dress other salads.

• •

A take on the 1980s shrimp cocktail salad. If you aren't a fan of mayonnaise, make the dressing with crème fraîche or whole Greek yogurt.

shrimp cocktail salad
with avocado

prep time: 10 minutes   **cook time:** 7 minutes   **serves:** 2

1 tablespoon olive oil

8 king shrimp, heads and shells on

2 garlic cloves, sliced

1 red chile, diced

1 handful of shredded iceberg lettuce

1 to 2 ripe tomatoes, diced

½ cucumber, diced

1 avocado, pitted and cubed

1 small box of watercress

Dressing

zest and juice of ½ lemon

½ teaspoon cayenne pepper

1 heaped teaspoon ketchup

3 tablespoons mayonnaise

Add the olive oil to a large skillet and place over high heat. Add the shrimp and cook for 4 minutes, then add the garlic and chile and fry and toss for another 3 minutes, or until the shrimp are cooked through. Remove from the heat and set aside.

For the dressing, combine the lemon juice and zest with the remaining dressing ingredients in a bowl and set aside.

Add the shredded lettuce to a large bowl with the tomatoes, cucumber, and avocado. Drizzle over half the dressing and toss until everything is coated.

Divide the salad between two bowls and top with the shrimp, watercress, and extra dressing. Serve at once.

store/make it vegan
For a vegan option, pan-fry a sliced zucchini instead of the shrimp.

When tomatoes are at their best, what is more delicious than a summer salad? Top with anchovies when feeling a little extra special.

summer panzanella
with basil

prep time: 15 minutes   **cook time:** 0 minutes   **serves:** 2

14 ounces (400g) summer tomatoes
   mixed, coarsely chopped

2 tablespoons capers

1 tablespoon red wine vinegar

½ red onion, finely sliced

1 large handful of basil, leaves picked

4 tablespoons olive oil

1 large handful of Jar Croutons
   (page 200)

salt and freshly ground black pepper

Add all the ingredients to a large bowl, season well with salt and pepper, and let stand for 10 minutes.

Toss the salad and serve at once.

store/make it vegan
Make a double batch of the croutons and store in an airtight container for up to a week.

Charring the fruit in this sweet and spicy salad brings out all its flavor. Serve with a glass of wine and pretend you are on vacation.

grilled fruit salad
with arugula, almonds & pickled chiles

prep time: 5 minutes   **cook time:** 7 minutes   **serves:** 2

• •

2 apricots, halved and pitted

1 nectarine, halved and pitted

1 peach, halved and pitted

2 tablespoons Citrus Dressing (page 190)

1 small handful of almonds, sliced

1 large handful of arugula leaves

2 tablespoons Mexican-Infused Pickled Chiles, sliced (page 194)

1 ball of mozzarella, torn

1 handful of Jar Croutons (page 200)

• •

Set a large stovetop grill pan over high heat, arrange the fruit, cut-side down, on the pan, and char for 5 minutes, or until charred lines appear. Flip and char for 2 minutes on the other side. Remove and coarsely chop, then add to a large bowl.

Add the dressing to the bowl together with all the remaining ingredients. Toss well until everything is thoroughly combined and serve.

• •

store/make it vegan
For a vegan option, leave out the cheese.

This is our take on a classic Vietnamese street food salad.
If you don't eat pork, just use tofu or shrimp, as both
are delicious. If you can't find butterhead lettuce, iceberg
lettuce is also great. You can cook the pork on a
barbecue for extra flavor.

sharing platter

Vietnamese-style rice noodle salad

prep time: 15 minutes   cook time: 8 minutes   serves: 6

14 ounces (400g) vermicelli noodles

½ cup (120ml) white vinegar

½ cup (100g) white sugar

1 pound 2 ounces (500g) pork belly

2 tablespoons peanut oil

3 Thai chiles, chopped

5 garlic cloves, finely chopped

2 tablespoons soy sauce

3 tablespoons honey

4 tablespoons sesame seeds

4 red and yellow carrots

1 head of iceberg lettuce, shredded

1 cucumber, peeled into long strips

1 bunch of scallions, sliced

1 jar Thai Chile &
    Ginger Dressing (page 189)

1 bunch of mint, leaves picked

1 bunch of Thai basil, leaves picked

generous 1 cup (150g)
    toasted peanuts

salt

1. Cook the rice noodles according to the package directions, then rinse under cold running water and set aside.

2. Use a vegetable peeler to peel the carrots into long strips. Add the vinegar and sugar to a bowl and stir until the sugar has dissolved. Add 1 teaspoon salt and mix. Stir in the carrots and set aside.

3. Cut the pork into bite-size pieces. Heat a stovetop grill pan over high heat. Add the oil to a bowl, then add the chile, garlic, and pork and mix well.

4. Add the soy sauce, honey, and sesame seeds to the pork and mix until the pork until is coated all over.

5. Grill the pork for 2 minutes on each side, or until charred and golden. You may need to do this in two batches. Remove the pork and pile onto a large platter.

6. Add the cooked noodles, carrots, shredded lettuce, and cucumber strips to the serving platter in separate piles.

7. Pile the scallions onto one side of the platter, then add the cooked pork to the middle. Drizzle half of the dressing over the salad.

8. Serve with a plate of herbs, bowl of peanuts, and the remaining dressing, then let people build their own bowls, adding more dressing as they eat.

This salad is similar to a warm, speedy risotto-style dish. It's a very good way to use up a glut of summer tomatoes.

warm tomato salad
with orzo & anchovies

prep time: 15 minutes   **cook time:** 15 minutes   **serves:** 2

• •

2 tablespoons olive oil

1½ cups (150g) orzo

3 garlic cloves, sliced

14 ounces (400g) mixed ripe
   tomatoes, chopped

2 ounces (50g) canned anchovies in
   olive oil

1 teaspoon hot pepper flakes

zest and juice of 1 lemon

1 handful of Crispy Onions
   (page 197)

1 handful of basil leaves

• •

Preheat the oven to 400°F (200°C).

Add 1 teaspoon of the olive oil to a heavy-bottomed saucepan and place over medium heat. Add the orzo and toast for 3 to 5 minutes, or until lightly golden. Pour enough boiling water to fill the pan a third of the way up the sides and bring to a boil. Reduce the heat and simmer for 6 to 8 minutes.

Meanwhile, add the garlic, chopped tomatoes, remaining olive oil, the anchovies, hot pepper flakes, the lemon zest, and half of the juice to a roasting pan, and roast in the oven for 15 minutes.

Once the orzo is cooked, drain and toss the orzo into the tomatoes with the remaining lemon juice. Divide between two plates and sprinkle with the onions and basil leaves.

• •

store/make it vegan
For a vegan option, omit the anchovies. It will still be really delicious.

Cherries used in savory dishes are a revelation. Their sweet yet sharp fruit tang is perfect in this summery salad.

cherry & jalapeño salad
with Israeli couscous

prep time: 5 minutes   **cook time:** 10 minutes   **serves:** 2

• •

1 tablespoon olive oil

1 cup (200g) Israeli couscous

1 jalapeño chile, sliced

1 teaspoon sumac

7 ounces (200g) cherries, pitted
  and halved

1 handful of hazelnuts, toasted

1 handful of dill leaves

1 handful of parsley leaves

1 handful of cilantro leaves

2 tablespoons Za'atar Dressing
  (page 189)

• •

Add the olive oil to a medium saucepan and place over medium heat, then add the couscous and toast for a few minutes. Pour in generous 2 cups (500ml) boiling water and boil for 7 to 8 minutes. Drain and set aside.

Place all the remaining ingredients in a large bowl, then add the couscous and toss until everything is thoroughly combined and coated in the dressing. Serve at once.

• •

store/make it vegan
You can make this salad a few hours in advance, dressing it just before serving.

This raw chopped salad is a brilliant cooling, crunchy salad when it's hot outside. You can easily add a protein of your choice, if desired.

spicy chopped salad
with black beans & spicy herb dressing

prep time: 10 minutes   **cook time:** 0 minutes   **serves:** 2

• •

⅔ cup (100g) canned black beans

1 garlic clove, grated

3 tablespoons Spicy Herb Dressing (page 186)

½ cucumber, chopped

1 fresh corn on the cob, corn kernels sliced off

1 avocado, peeled, pitted, and chopped

1 handful of cherry tomatoes, halved

1 handful of little gem lettuce, sliced

1 red onion, diced

1 handful of chopped Mexican cheese of your choice

salt and freshly ground black pepper

• •

Place the beans in a large bowl with the grated garlic and one tablespoon of the dressing. Toss and season to taste.

Add piles of chopped cucumber, corn, avocado, cherry tomatoes, lettuce leaves, diced onion, and chopped cheese to two serving bowls and finish with a pile of beans and a good drizzle of the dressing.

• •

store/make it vegan

Omit the cheese or use a smoky vegan cheese substitute if making this salad vegan.

• •

This salad is packed with flavor. We use a crunchy chile oil (page 203), but if you don't have time to make it, buy a good-quality chile oil instead.

smashed cucumber salad
with jasmine rice

prep time: 5 minutes   **cook time:** 15 minutes   **serves:** 2

¾ cup (150g) jasmine rice

1 large cucumber

1 tablespoon superfine sugar

1 garlic clove, grated

2-inch (5-cm) piece ginger, peeled and julienned

2 tablespoons Chinkiang black rice vinegar

1 large handful of cilantro, leaves and stems chopped

3 tablespoons Asian-Infused Hot Crunchy Oil (page 203)

1 handful of pea shoots

salt and freshly ground black pepper

Rinse the rice and cook according to the package directions in a rice cooker.

Cut the cucumber lengthwise and use a spoon to remove the seeds. Place the cucumber on a cutting board, cut-side down, and bash it slightly with a rolling pin, then cut into three chunks on the bias.

Add the warm rice to a large bowl and toss in all the remaining ingredients, except for the pea shoots. Taste and adjust the seasoning, if needed. Serve with a sprinkling of pea shoots and eat at once.

store/make it vegan
For a more substantial vegan salad, sprinkle with pumpkin seeds and chopped almonds just before serving.

This salad has lots of flavor, color, and crunch. We use crispy torn pitas, but if you have store-bought crispy croutons use them instead.

za'atar fattoush
with crispy pita toppers

prep time: 10 minutes   **cook time:** 8 minutes   **serves:** 2

• •

2 pitas

1 tablespoon olive oil

1 tablespoon sumac

1 cucumber, diced

10 mixed tomatoes, coarsely chopped

1 red bell pepper, diced

1 red onion, sliced into half-moons

1 head of little gem lettuce, sliced

1 large handful of chopped
   flat-leaf parsley

1 large handful of chopped mint

1 handful of pomegranate seeds

zest and juice of ½ lemon

2 tablespoons Za'atar Dressing
   (page 189)

salt and freshly ground black pepper

• •

Preheat the oven to 400°F (200°C).

Tear the pitas into bite-size chunks, tearing them apart so you have single layers of pita. Add the pita chunks to a large baking sheet, then drizzle with the olive oil and toss until coated. Season with salt and pepper and sprinkle with the sumac. Toast in the oven for 8 minutes, or until golden and crisp, tossing and checking every few minutes. Once cooked, remove from the oven and set aside.

Add the cucumber, tomatoes, bell pepper, red onion, lettuce, herbs, pomegranate seeds, and crispy pita to two bowls. Add the lemon zest and juice, then season with salt and pepper. Drizzle over the dressing and serve at once.

• •

store/make it vegan
You can toast the pitas a couple of hours in advance, if desired.

• •

Sweet, ripe tomatoes, creamy mild ricotta, and fresh herbs are a dream combination. Serve with crusty bread for a light lunch.

summer tomato salad

with crispy pangrattato & whipped ricotta

prep time: 5 minutes   **cook time:** 0 minutes   **serves:** 2

• •

scant 1 cup (200g) ricotta

1 bunch of parsley, chopped

14 ounces (400g) ripe tomatoes,
   coarsely chopped

2 tablespoons olive oil

1 tablespoon red wine vinegar

2 ounces (50g) canned good-quality
   anchovies in olive oil, drained

1 handful of marjoram or
   oregano leaves

3 tablespoons Pangrattato Crumb
   (page 201)

salt

• •

Blitz the ricotta and parsley in a food processor or blender until smooth and pale green. Season with salt.

Scoop the ricotta mixture out and spread over a large serving plate. Top with the chopped tomatoes, drizzle over the olive oil and vinegar, then top with the anchovies, marjoram, and pangrattato crumb. Serve at once.

• •

store/make it vegan
You can blitz the ricotta and parsley in advance and store in the refrigerator until ready to assemble the salad.

Sev is a popular Indian deep-fried snack consisting of crispy noodles made from chickpea flour. Omit it if you can't find it.

Indian-style chaat salad
with cilantro & tamarind sauces

prep time: 10 minutes   **cook time:** 20 minutes   **serves:** 2

• •

2 potatoes, peeled and cubed

¾ cup (100g) garbanzo beans

2 tablespoons ghee or oil

1 lemon, chopped and juice of 1 lime

1 tablespoon garam masala

2 teaspoons chaat masala

1 teaspoon ground cumin

1 large bunch of cilantro

2 small green Thai chiles

½ cucumber, chopped

4 tomatoes, chopped

1 red onion, diced

1 handful of pomegranate seeds

2 tablespoons tamarind sauce

1 handful of sev (optional)

salt

• •

Preheat the oven to 400°F (200°C).

Add the potatoes and garbanzo beans to a medium baking sheet, then add the ghee, chopped lemon, and garam masala, and toss well. Roast in the oven for 20 minutes, tossing halfway through. (Roasting the lemon makes the peel very soft and tender.)

Remove the potatoes and beans from the oven and toss in the chaat masala and cumin.

Place the cilantro, green chiles, lime juice, and 1 tablespoon water in a small blender and season with salt. Blitz until it is smooth and a vivid green color.

Add the chopped cucumber, tomatoes, red onion, and pomegranate seeds to the potatoes and mix well. Scoop into a serving bowl, then drizzle over the cilantro and tamarind sauces. Finish with sev, if using, and serve at once.

• •

store/make it vegan
You can roast the potatoes and garbanzo beans and toss them in the spices a couple of hours in advance, if desired, then assemble the rest of the salad before serving.

• •

A take on a classic Thai dish, this is flavorful and moreish. You can also serve these in iceberg lettuce cups if you can't find little gem.

Thai pork larb salad

with all the summer herbs

prep time: 10 minutes   **cook time:** 20 minutes   **serves:** 2

2 tablespoons sticky rice

1 tablespoon peanut oil

4 shallots, sliced

9 ounces (250g) ground pork

1 lemongrass stalk, sliced

6 makrut lime leaves, thinly sliced

2 small red Thai chiles, thinly sliced

3 garlic cloves, thinly sliced

juice of 1 lime

1 tablespoon fish sauce

2 heads of little gem lettuce

1 small bunch each of cilantro, Thai
   basil, and mint leaves

1 jar Thai Chile & Ginger
   Dressing (page 189)

salt

Place a large wok over high heat, add the rice, and toast for 10 minutes, or until golden all over. Remove the rice and grind in a mortar and pestle to a coarse powder.

Add the oil to the wok and fry the shallots over medium heat for 1 minute. Add the pork, lemongrass, makrut lime leaves, chiles, and garlic and fry over high heat for another 10 minutes tossing frequently. Add the ground rice, lime juice, and fish sauce to season, then taste and add salt, if needed.

Separate the lettuce into leaves, then place the leaves on a platter and scoop the pork into the cups. Sprinkle with the herbs and serve with the dressing to dip your cups in.

store/make it vegan
Roast the pork ahead of time and then reheat before serving, if desired.

salad in a jar

Cold carrot noodle salad

with poached chicken & summer herbs

prep time: 10 minutes   **cook time:** 10 minutes   **serves:** 2

• •

2 chicken breasts

1 lemon, sliced

1 small bunch of tarragon

2 large carrots

1 large zucchini

1 handful of toasted pine nuts

1 handful of basil leaves

1 handful of mint leaves

1 handful of pitted black
  olives, halved

3 tablespoons Citrus Dressing
  (page 190)

• •

Bring a medium saucepan of water to a boil, add the chicken breasts, sliced lemon, and tarragon, and reduce the heat to a simmer. (Cooking the lemon makes the peel very soft and tender.) Cover with a lid and simmer for 10 minutes, or until the chicken is perfectly cooked. Remove the chicken from the water with a spatula and let cool slightly.

Using a spiralizer, make noodles of the carrots and zucchini and pile into the bottom of two 17-ounce (500-ml) mason jars. Add a layer of pine nuts followed by the herbs. Slice the chicken and add to the jars with the olives. When ready to eat, top the jars with the dressing, close the jars with the lid, and give them a good shake.

• •

store/make it vegan
For a vegan option, use roasted cauliflower instead of the chicken and use maple syrup instead of honey in the dressing.

• •

This salad is perfect for those balmy summer days or nights. If it's super hot outside, keep the melon cold in the refrigerator before chopping.

melon & prosciutto salad
with pangrattato & citrus dressing

prep time: 5 minutes   **cook time:** 0 minutes   **serves:** 2

• •

½ ripe melon of your choice (we
    used Orange Candy)

6 strips of prosciutto

1 handful of mint leaves

1 handful of basil leaves

½ red onion, thinly sliced

1 handful of Pangrattato Crumb
    (page 201)

1 tablespoon Citrus Dressing
    (page 190)

1 tablespoon extra-virgin olive oil

salt and freshly ground black pepper

• •

Peel and slice the melon into thin wedges and place on two serving plates or a platter.

Drape the prosciutto over the melon and sprinkle over the herbs, onion, and pangrattato crumb. Drizzle with the dressing and olive oil. Season with salt and pepper and serve.

• •

store/make it vegan
If you don't eat meat, simply leave it out and sprinkle with nuts or seeds of your choice. Swap the honey in the dressing for maple syrup.

• •

Serve this classic Greek salad with barbecued meat or vegetables. If you happen to have any left over, then blitz and serve as a cold soup.

the ultimate Greek salad

with black olives, feta & oregano

prep time: 10 minutes   **cook time:** 0 minutes   **serves:** 2

• •

1 pound 2 ounces (500g) mixed
   tomatoes, coarsely chopped

1 small red onion, sliced

½ cucumber, chopped

1 handful of mint leaves

1 large handful of black olives, pitted

1 tablespoon red wine vinegar

3 tablespoons extra-virgin olive oil

7 ounces (200g) block of feta

2 teaspoons dried oregano

salt and freshly ground black pepper

• •

Mix the tomatoes, onion, cucumber, mint, and olives together in a large bowl. Add the vinegar and olive oil and toss until everything is coated. Season with salt and pepper.

Divide the salad between two plates. Sprinkle the feta generously with oregano, then add to the plates and serve.

• •

store/make it vegan
For a vegan option, either use store-bought vegan feta or toss through some canned garbanzo beans, if desired.

• •

This is a variation of a tuna Niçoise salad. For perfect yolks, cook the eggs for six minutes, but if you like yours hard, cook for two extra minutes.

a kinda Niçoise salad

with Dijon dressing

prep time: 5 minutes   **cook time:** 15 minutes   **serves:** 2

· ·

1 handful of baby potatoes, halved

1 handful of green beans, halved

2 eggs

1 handful of chopped black olives

½ red onion, finely sliced

1 bunch of parsley leaves

½ cucumber, sliced

7½ ounces (220g) jarred good-quality
  tuna in olive oil

2 tablespoons Dijon Dressing
  (page 187)

salt and freshly ground black pepper

· ·

Fill a small saucepan with water and bring to a boil. Add the potatoes and boil for 6 minutes, or until soft when pierced with a knife. Remove the potatoes with a slotted spoon and add to a salad bowl. Return the pan and cooking water to the heat.

Add the green beans to the boiling water and boil for 1 minute, then scoop out and add to the potatoes in the bowl.

Add the eggs to the cooking water and boil for 6 minutes, or until soft-boiled. Once done, drain and rinse under cold running water to stop them cooking any further. Peel the eggs and slice in half. Set aside.

Add the olives, onion, parsley, cucumber, tuna, and dressing to the potatoes and beans and toss together, then divide between two bowls. Top with the egg and season with salt and pepper.

· ·

store/make it vegan
You can make this salad in advance and dress just before eating.

· ·

What's not to love about coffee and vanilla mascarpone and sweet fruit on a warm evening? Use whatever summer fruit is at its best.

summer fruit salad

with a coffee mascarpone

prep time: 10 minutes   **cook time:** 0 minutes   **serves:** 2

1 handful of cherries, pitted
  and sliced

1 handful of strawberries, hulled
  and halved

2 plums, pitted and sliced

1 nectarine, pitted and sliced

2 tablespoons maple syrup

juice of 1 lemon

1 teaspoon vanilla bean paste

1 tablespoon camp coffee

scant ½ cup (100g) mascarpone

1 handful of mint leaves

Place the fruit in a medium bowl, then add half the maple syrup and lemon juice and toss until the fruit is coated. Let marinate.

Using a balloon whisk, whisk the remaining maple syrup, vanilla, coffee, and mascarpone together in a large bowl until smooth and thick.

Divide the fruit between two bowls and top with the mascarpone. Drizzle any juices over and finish with a sprinkling of mint. Serve at once.

store/make it vegan

You can make both the salad and mascarpone in advance and chill in the refrigerator until ready to serve.

fall

• •

seasonal veggies fall

leaves

kale

In the fall, kale has a sweeter and nuttier flavor, so is very well suited to warming salads containing squash, pumpkins, Brussels sprouts, apples, and nuts.

lettuce

There are lots of varieties of lettuce in the fall, including Romaine and little gem, which when combined with foods such as butternut squash, can make hearty salads.

arugula

Arugula has a peppery flavor, which goes so well with foods associated with fall, such as butternut squash, apples, beets, oranges, and pears. Try the Brussels Sprouts Salad on page 113.

chicory

Chicory, such as Belgian endive, radicchio, and escarole, has a strong bitter taste and pairs well with other fall foods, such as pears, oranges, nuts, and apples.

Tuscan kale

Tuscan kale, or cavolo nero, has a sweeter and milder flavor than other kales so pairs well with other fall foods, such as beets, leeks, and carrots.

roots

wild

carrots

Carrots become the star of fall salads as their sweetness complements the bitterness of other foods such as chicory, arugula, and parsley.

radishes

Fall and winter radishes, such as the watermelon radish, have a mild, peppery flavor and are delicious eaten raw or cooked with beets and apples.

new potatoes

Potatoes, including new potatoes, pair well with other foods we associate with fall, such as squash, Brussels sprouts, kale, and sweet potatoes.

turnips

Turnips are quite mild when raw but have a sweeter, earthier, and nuttier flavor when cooked, which goes well with other fall foods including carrots, potatoes, and apples.

mushrooms

Mushrooms excel in the fall. Their earthy and meaty flavor goes well with other fall foods, such as onions, garlic, nuts, and greens. Try the Wild Mushroom Salad on page 115.

kitchen garden

avocados
Ripe avocados have a sweet and nutty taste, which goes well with other foods we associate with fall including walnuts, butternut squash, and pears.

squash
From butternut squash to acorn squash, there are so many varieties available from fall. Their earthy and nutty taste pairs well with mushrooms, Brussels sprouts, and apples.

celery
Celery has a strong but mild flavor and makes a good addition to hearty fall salads, alongside parsley, celery root, leeks, and apples. Try the leek salad on page 145.

leeks
Leeks have a mild, sweet flavor, which goes well with other foods we associate with fall, such as apples, potatoes, mushrooms, thyme, and cheese.

cauliflower
Cauliflower has a nutty taste with bitter undertones and is an ideal ingredient to add to hearty salads, together with nuts, cilantro, squash, and garbanzo beans.

fruit

pears
Pears come into their own in the fall. Their mild, sweet, and earthy taste goes with other foods, such as apples, squashes, potatoes, and walnuts. Try the Pear & Chicory Salad on page 131.

apples
There are so many apple varieties and flavors, from sweet and crunchy to tart, and they go well with other fall foods including beets, squash, cabbage, kale, and pears.

figs
Fall figs are sweet with a honeylike flavor and a soft texture, which pairs well with walnuts, cheese, plums, and grapes. Try the Roasted Fall Fruit salad on page 123.

plums
Plums are another fall fruit. With a mild, sweet, and tart flavor, and juicy flesh, plums go with cheese, nuts, ginger, cinnamon, honey, and apples.

blackberries
Ripe, juicy blackberries have a sweet, slightly tart flavor and pair well with other fall foods including apples, nuts, pumpkin seeds, cinnamon, and ginger.

charred onion salad

with broiled lamb chops

prep time: 5 minutes   **cook time:** 15 minutes   **serves:** 2

• •

4 lamb chops

1 tablespoon olive oil

1 tablespoon Turkish red
   pepper flakes

2 teaspoons fennel seeds

2 teaspoons coriander seeds

2 teaspoons ground cumin

3 red onions, quartered

1 handful of pomegranate seeds

2 teaspoons ground sumac

1 bunch of mint leaves

1 bunch of parsley

2 tablespoons pomegranate molasses

juice of 1 lemon

salt and freshly ground black pepper

• •

Heat a broiler to high or a barbecue, if using.

Place the lamb chops in a large bowl, then add the olive oil, Turkish pepper, fennel seeds, coriander seeds, and ground cumin. Season with salt and pepper, then turn the chops so they are coated in the mixture.

Arrange the onions on a large baking sheet and broil for 5 minutes, or until slightly charred. Turn the onions over, add the chops to the baking sheet, and broil for another 5 minutes.

Meanwhile, add the remaining ingredients to a large salad bowl.

Turn the chops and onions over and broil for another 5 minutes.

Remove the chops and onions from the broiler and add the onions to the salad bowl and mix. Pile the salad onto two plates, top with the chops, and serve.

• •

store/make it vegan
If you don't eat meat, then use charred smoked tofu broiled in the same way.

• •

This fall fruit salad is very easy and really quick to make for breakfast or a healthy dessert. Choose your favorite variety of apple and pear.

apple & pear salad
with whipped ricotta

prep time: 10 minutes   **cook time:** 0 minutes   **serves:** 2

scant 1 cup (200g) ricotta
zest and juice of ½ orange
2 tablespoons runny honey
1 pear, sliced into matchsticks
1 Pink Lady apple, sliced
  into matchsticks
1 handful of blackberries, sliced

1 handful of toasted hazelnuts,
  coarsely chopped
1 handful of toasted coconut flakes

Whisk the ricotta, orange zest, juice, and honey together in a medium bowl.

Spread the ricotta across two bowls and top with the fruit, nuts, and coconut flakes. Serve at once.

store/make it vegan
You can whisk the ricotta ahead of time and assemble the salad just before eating.

The spicy dressing tossed through all the greens and finished with salmon is a dream. Use whatever crunchy greens you have in the refrigerator.

roast salmon salad

with crunchy greens

prep time: 10 minutes   **cook time:** 10 minutes   **serves:** 2

2 x 5½-ounce (150-g) skinless
   salmon fillets

1 tablespoon olive oil

1 lemon, sliced

1 avocado, pitted and cubed

2 celery stalks, sliced

1 head of little gem lettuce, shredded

1 handful of sugar snap peas, halved

1 handful of watercress

1 handful of dill leaves

2 tablespoons Green Goddess
   Jalapeño Dressing (page 188)

salt and freshly ground black pepper

3 tablespoons Umami Toasted Seeds
   (page 196), for garnish

Preheat the oven to 480°F (250°C).

Lay the salmon on a small baking sheet, drizzle over the olive oil, and top each fillet with lemon slices. Season the fillets with salt and pepper and roast in the oven for 10 minutes. (Roasting the lemon makes the peel very soft and tender.)

Place the avocado, celery, lettuce, sugar snap peas, watercress, and dill in a large bowl. Add the dressing and toss until everything is coated. Pile onto two plates.

When cooked, flake the salmon over the salad and garnish with the toasted seeds. Serve at once.

store/make it vegan

For a vegan option, instead of the salmon, cut a butternut squash into cubes and roast in the oven for 20 minutes, or until tender.

This hearty salad gives Brussels sprouts their moment to shine. Crunchy sprouts with salty feta and peppery arugula is a perfect combo.

Brussels sprouts salad
with parsley & Dijon dressing

prep time: 5 minutes   **cook time:** 10 minutes   **serves:** 2

• •

1 tablespoon olive oil

7 ounces (200g) Brussels
   sprouts, halved

1 bunch of parsley leaves

3 tablespoons Dijon Dressing
   (page 187)

2 tablespoons pine nuts, toasted

1 small handful of toasted
   almonds, chopped

2 handfuls of arugula leaves

3½ ounces (100g) feta, crumbled
   into pieces

• •

Place a large skillet over high heat, add the olive oil, then place the Brussels sprouts, cut-side down, in the pan. Fry for 6 minutes, or until deep golden on that side. Flip the Brussels sprouts over and fry for another 4 minutes.

Blitz the parsley and dressing together in a small blender until vivid green.

Tip the Brussels sprouts into a large bowl and add the pine nuts, almonds, arugula, and feta. Add the dressing and toss until everything is coated. Serve.

• •

store/make it vegan

To make this vegan, omit the feta and fry some cubes of marinated tofu, then sprinkle them over the finished dish. Use maple syrup instead of honey in the dressing.

• •

This season the mushrooms are delicious, so use any mushrooms you love or whatever is at its best. Be sure to fry them until golden brown.

wild mushroom salad
with a poached egg

prep time: 10 minutes   **cook time:** 15 minutes   **serves:** 2

• •

1 tablespoon olive oil	1 large bunch of parsley
1 tablespoon butter	1 large handful of arugula leaves
14 ounces (400g) mixed wild mushrooms, large ones halved	¾ ounce (20g) Parmesan, shaved (optional)
3 garlic cloves, sliced	1 handful of Jar Croutons (page 200)
juice of ½ lemon	2 tablespoons Chile Dressing (page 191), optional
2 eggs	
pinch of hot pepper flakes	salt and freshly ground black pepper

• •

Place a large skillet over high heat, add the olive oil and butter, then add the larger mushrooms and fry for 5 minutes. Add the smaller mushrooms and fry for another 5 minutes. Add the sliced garlic and fry for 2 to 3 minutes until all the mushrooms and garlic are golden. Add the lemon juice and season with salt and pepper.

Meanwhile, bring a medium saucepan of water to a boil over high heat. Break the eggs into the boiling water and poach for 3 to 4 minutes until the whites are set and the yolks are still runny. Scoop out the eggs with a slotted spoon and drain on a plate.

Remove the mushrooms from the heat, add the hot pepper flakes, parsley, and arugula, and toss until everything is well combined.

Divide between two bowls and top with the poached eggs, shaved Parmesan, if using, the croutons, and the dressing, if using. Serve.

• •

store/make it vegan
Make a double or treble batch of croutons and store in an airtight container for a week, sprinkling over other salads.

• •

Squash is at its best in the fall—sweet, delicate, and very filling. This salad makes for a perfect warm, comforting meal in cooler months.

roasted squash salad

with crispy sage

prep time: 5 minutes   **cook time:** 45 minutes   **serves:** 2

• •

1 cup (150g) spelt grains

1 small onion squash

2 red onions, quartered

2 tablespoons olive oil

1 tablespoon butter

2 handfuls of sage leaves

1 preserved lemon, chopped

2 handfuls of watercress

3 tablespoons Umami Toasted Seeds
  (page 196)

1 teaspoon sumac

salt and freshly ground black pepper

• •

Preheat the oven to 400°F (200°C).

Add the spelt to a medium saucepan, pour in generous 2 cups (500ml) water, and place over high heat. Season with salt, then once boiling, reduce the heat to low, cover with a lid, and simmer for 45 minutes, or until chewy but not crunchy.

Meanwhile, cut the squash in half, scoop out the seeds and discard. Cut the squash into thin boats and place on a large baking sheet. Add the onions and drizzle over 1 tablespoon of the oil. Season well with salt and pepper and roast for 15 minutes.

Meanwhile, heat the butter in a skillet over medium heat, add the sage, and fry for 3 minutes, or until crisp. Scoop onto a plate and set aside.

Flip the squash over and roast for another 10 minutes, or until soft and golden.

Drain the spelt, add to a platter, drizzle with the remaining oil, and add the lemon. Season to taste. Add the watercress and top with the squash, onions, seeds, and sumac.

• •

store/make it vegan
This salad can be easily made in advance and served cold.

• •

This crunchy, spicy, and refreshing salad is packed full of flavor. If you can't find sushi-grade tuna, use hot-smoked salmon fillets instead.

Japanese turnip salad
with raw tuna, roasted seeds & miso dressing

prep time: 5 minutes   **cook time:** 0 minutes   **serves:** 2

• •

1 bunch of Japanese turnips

1 baby cucumber, sliced

1 bunch of cilantro leaves (optional)

8 shiso leaves, torn

3½ ounces (100g) sushi-grade tuna, diced

1 jalapeño chile, sliced

1 tablespoon Asian-Infused Hot Crunchy oil (page 203)

2 tablespoons Miso & Lime Dressing (page 188)

2 tablespoons Umami Toasted Seeds (page 196)

• •

Using a sharp knife or a mandoline, finely slice the turnips and add to a large bowl.

Add all the remaining ingredients to the bowl, then toss until everything is well combined and serve at once.

• •

store/make it vegan
For a vegan option, good-quality silken tofu works well instead of the tuna.

• •

This is a heavily dressed salad but it's up to you how much dressing to add. We added rye croutons to bulk it up but it's delicious served with salmon.

classic Waldorf salad
with spiced rye bread & walnut crumb

prep time: 15 minutes   **cook time:** 0 minutes   **serves:** 2

3½ tablespoons mayonnaise

3½ tablespoons Greek yogurt

1 teaspoon English mustard

6 tarragon sprigs, finely chopped

juice of 1 lemon

1¾ ounces (50g) Rye-Baked
   Croutons (page 199)

scant ½ cup (60g) walnuts, toasted

3½ ounces (100g) green
   grapes, sliced

2 celery stalks, cut into ¾-inch
   (2-cm) chunks

2 Pippin apples, cut into matchsticks

1 romaine lettuce, coarsely chopped

salt and freshly ground black pepper

Start by making the dressing, Place the mayonnaise, yogurt, and mustard into a bowl and whisk well. Add the tarragon and lemon juice and mix well, then season to taste.

Blitz the rye croutons and toasted walnuts in a food processor until it is a coarse crumb. Set aside.

Add the grapes, celery, apples, and lettuce to a salad bowl, add the dressing, and give it a really good mix until everything is combined.

Divide the salad between two plates and top with the rye and walnut crumb. Serve.

store/make it vegan
Make the dressing in advance and store it in the refrigerator until you are ready to assemble the rest of the salad. You can make the rye and walnut crumb ahead of time too.

This warm roasted fruit salad is very versatile—eat it for breakfast with a dollop of yogurt or even as a dessert with some ice cream.

roasted fall fruit salad

with a spiced oat crumb

prep time: 10 minutes   **cook time:** 10 minutes   **serves:** 2

• •

2 pears, quartered

2 figs, halved

2 plums, quartered

1 handful of green grapes

1 handful of almonds

3½ tablespoons maple syrup

zest and juice of 1 orange

2 tablespoons butter

1 ball of preserved ginger, chopped

½ cup (50g) jumbo oats

½ teaspoon ground cinnamon

• •

Preheat the oven to 400°F (200°C).

Add the chopped pears, figs, plums, grapes, almonds, maple syrup, and orange juice to a small sheet pan and roast in the oven for 10 minutes.

Meanwhile, add the butter, chopped preserved ginger, oats, orange zest, and cinnamon to a medium skillet and place over medium heat. Fry for 5 to 8 minutes, or until golden and crisp.

Divide the spiced oat crumb between two bowls and top with the roasted fruit. Serve.

• •

store/make it vegan

The fruit can be made ahead and served cold, or add it to oatmeal for a filling breakfast.

• •

This take on a Caesar salad is delicious as the raw Brussels sprouts give it an earthy taste. If using a mandoline, be careful of your fingers.

Brussels Caesar salad
with rye croutons & watercress

prep time: 10 minutes   **cook time:** 0 minutes   **serves:** 2

• •

14 ounces (400g) Brussels sprouts

juice of ½ lemon

1 tablespoon olive oil

1 handful of watercress

1 handful of toasted
   almonds, chopped

1 avocado, halved, pitted,
   and chopped

3 tablespoons Parmesan Dressing
   (page 186)

1 handful of Rye-Baked Croutons
   (page 199)

salt and freshly ground black pepper

• •

Using a sharp knife or a mandoline, finely slice the Brussels sprouts into a large bowl. Add the lemon juice and drizzle over the olive oil. Toss it really well, then season generously with salt and pepper.

Add all the remaining ingredients to the bowl, then serve at once.

• •

store/make it vegan
Make the dressing with vegan yogurt, swap the cheese for 2 tablespoons of nutritional yeast, and omit the anchovies.

• •

This potato salad is perfect eaten warm, but you can also eat it cold if you are on the move. If you don't love spice, then omit the chile.

a perfect potato salad
with capers & crème fraîche

prep time: 5 minutes   **cook time:** 20 minutes   **serves:** 2

• •

10½ ounces (300g) new potatoes, larger potatoes halved

1¾ ounces (50g) diced pancetta

2 handfuls of Tuscan kale, finely shredded

1 tablespoon olive oil

zest and juice of ½ lemon

1 red chile, diced

2 tablespoons capers

3 dill pickles, chopped

1 handful of dill leaves, plus extra

1 handful of chives, chopped

1 handful of parsley, chopped

scant 1 cup (200g) crème fraîche

olive oil, for drizzling (optional)

salt and freshly ground black pepper

• •

Bring the potatoes to a boil in a saucepan of salted water. Once boiling, reduce the heat and simmer for 10 to 15 minutes, or until the potatoes are soft all the way through.

Meanwhile, fry the pancetta in a large skillet over medium heat for 5 minutes. Add the kale, olive oil, lemon zest and juice, the chile, and capers and fry for another 4 minutes.

Once the potatoes are cooked, drain and tip into a salad bowl. Add the pickles, herbs, and crème fraîche and season generously with salt and pepper. Fold through the pancetta and kale mixture and top with some extra dill and some olive oil, if desired.

• •

store/make it vegan
To make this vegan, omit the pancetta and swap the crème fraîche for vegan mayonnaise.

What's not to love here?—salty, fried halloumi with crunchy green beans and tomatoes. This is great served with baked fish and charred meat.

halloumi & bean salad

with black olives & pistachios

prep time: 5 minutes   **cook time:** 10 minutes   **serves:** 2

1 teaspoon olive oil

8-ounce (225-g) block of halloumi, cut into cubes

10½ ounces (300g) green beans, halved

1 tablespoon mustard seeds

zest and juice of 1 lemon

3 tablespoons pitted black olives, halved

4 large tomatoes, chopped

1 handful of toasted pistachios, chopped

1 handful of mint leaves

1 tablespoon honey (optional)

Mix the olive oil and halloumi together in a medium bowl until the halloumi is coated all over in the oil.

Place a large skillet over medium heat, add the halloumi, and fry for 1 minute on each side, or until golden all over.

Add the green beans, mustard seeds, and lemon zest and juice, and fry for 2 minutes. Tip into a salad bowl with the olives, tomatoes, pistachios, and mint, then finish with a drizzle of honey, if desired. Serve.

store/make it vegan

For a vegan option, use a block of firm tofu or marinated tofu instead of the halloumi and swap the honey for maple syrup.

This salad makes the most of what's in season. If you don't like gorgonzola, a soft goat cheese or even feta works well.

pear & chicory salad

with gorgonzola, hazelnut & chile dressing

prep time: 5 minutes   **cook time:** 6 minutes   **serves:** 2

• •

1 tablespoon butter

2 pears, quartered and cored

juice of ½ lemon

2 heads of chicory, leaves separated

1 handful of watercress

1 handful of toasted
   hazelnuts, chopped

1¾ ounces (50g) gorgonzola

2 tablespoons Chile Dressing
   (page 191)

• •

Add the butter to a large skillet and place over medium heat. Add the pears and lemon juice and fry for 2 to 3 minutes until golden brown. Flip the pears over and fry the other side for another 2 to 3 minutes.

Meanwhile, add the chicory leaves, watercress, hazelnuts, and gorgonzola to a salad bowl. Pour in the dressing and toss until everything is coated in the dressing.

Arrange the fried pears across two plates and top with the salad.

• •

store/make it vegan
You can fry the pears in advance and then assemble the rest of the salad before eating.

• •

salad in a jar

Packed full of earthy fall flavors, and finished with creamy ricotta, this salad makes a great jar lunch—dress just before eating.

perfect fall salad

with toasted seeds & citrus dressing

prep time: 20 minutes   **cook time:** 0 minutes   **serves:** 2

• •

4 celery stalks, sliced on the bias

7 ounces (200g) Brussels sprouts, finely shredded

3 apples, cut into matchsticks

1 head of kale, finely sliced

¾ cup (100g) smoked roasted almonds, chopped

1 handful of tarragon, chopped

1 handful of dill, chopped

½ jar Umami Toasted Seeds (page 196)

⅓ cup (50g) toasted mixed seeds, we used pumpkin and sesame

scant ½ cup (100g) ricotta

1 jar Citrus Dressing (page 190)

• •

Add the celery to the bottom of two 34-ounce (1-liter) mason jars, then add the Brussels sprouts in another layer, followed by the apple, sliced kale, smoked almonds, chopped herbs, and toasted seeds. Divide the ricotta equally between both jars. When ready to eat, pour over the dressing, close the lid, and give it a good shake.

• •

store/make it vegan
To make this vegan, use good-quality silken tofu instead of the ricotta, or add extra smoked almonds, if desired.

For those lovers of buffalo wings, this is your salad. We have used cauliflower to bulk it up and keep it a little healthier, then finished it with lots of crunchy celery and a cooling blue cheese. This salad won't stand around for long, so make and eat it at once.

sharing platter

buffalo cauliflower blue cheese salad

prep time: 10 minutes   **cook time:** 20 minutes   **serves:** 6

••

2 large cauliflowers, about 3 pounds 5 ounces (1.5kg), coarsely chopped

generous 1 cup (150g) rice flour

1 tablespoon garlic powder

1¾ cups (400ml) cold fizzy water

1 stick minus 1 tablespoon (100g) butter

scant 1 cup (200ml) Frank's red hot buffalo sauce

1 lemon

1 head celery, sliced on the bias, leaves kept for garnish

3-ounce (80-g) bag of watercress

3½ ounces (100g) blue cheese, plus extra for serving

salt and freshly ground black pepper

1. Preheat the oven to 425°F (220°C). Chop the cauliflower into large florets and set aside.

2. Add the rice flour and garlic powder to a large bowl and whisk in the fizzy water. Season with salt and pepper and toss in the cauliflower.

3. Line a large sheet pan with baking parchment and tip the cauliflower onto the lined sheet. Bake in the oven for 20 minutes, or until golden and crispy, making sure to toss the cauliflower halfway through.

4. Meanwhile, make the buffalo sauce. Melt the butter in a small saucepan over low heat. Add the hot buffalo sauce and mix with a wooden spoon until well combined. Remove from the heat and set aside.

5. Squeeze the lemon juice into the sauce and taste, adjusting the seasoning if needed with salt and pepper.

6. Once the cauliflower is done, tip it onto a serving platter and drizzle over most of the buffalo sauce, setting the rest aside for serving.

7. Top the cauliflower with the celery and watercress, then sprinkle over the blue cheese and reserved celery leaves.

8. Serve at once with the remaining sauce and extra blue cheese for guests to help themselves.

Not only is this salad a joy to look at, but it's filled with flavor and texture. If you don't eat fish, it works well with broiled chicken or baked feta.

radish & salmon salad

with lots of herbs & citrus dressing

prep time: 5 minutes **cook time:** 12 minutes **serves:** 2

• •

2 x 5-ounce (140-g) salmon fillets

1 lemon, sliced

7 ounces (200g) broccolini, halved

2 garlic cloves, finely sliced

1 teaspoon olive oil

3 watermelon radishes

1 jalapeño chile

2 tablespoons Citrus Dressing
 (page 190)

salt and freshly ground black pepper

2 tablespoons Umami Toasted Seeds
 (page 196), for garnish

• •

Preheat the oven to 425°F (220°C).

Lay the salmon, skin-side down, on one side of a medium baking sheet. Season with salt and pepper and top with the sliced lemon. Add the broccolini to the other side of the baking sheet with the sliced garlic. Drizzle with the olive oil, season, and roast in the oven for 12 minutes, tossing the broccolini halfway through.

Using a mandoline, finely slice the watermelon radishes and chile and add to a large bowl. Add the dressing and toss until the radishes are coated in the dressing.

When the salmon is cooked, toss the broccolini into the radish bowl and divide between two plates. Top with the salmon, flaked into pieces, and garnish with toasted seeds. Serve at once.

• •

store/make it vegan
Panko-crumbed fried tofu is a great alternative if you are vegan, and use maple syrup instead of honey in the dressing.

• •

This salad is finished with creamy burrata, and is the perfect pairing with the carrots. Keep the pickling liquid and use to pickle other veg.

pickled carrot salad
with herbs, toasted seeds & za'atar dressing

prep time: 5 minutes   **cook time:** 15 minutes   **serves:** 2

• •

2 bunches of baby carrots, halved

1½ cups (300ml) white wine vinegar

¾ cup (150g) superfine sugar

½ cup (30g) salt

2 red chiles, sliced

1 handful of mint, parsley, and
   dill leaves

1 burrata

1½ cups (200g) canned garbanzo
   beans, rinsed and drained

2 tablespoons Za'atar Dressing
   (page 189)

• •

Place the carrots in a wide saucepan, then add the vinegar, sugar, salt, sliced chile, and ⅔ cup (150ml) water. Bring to a boil over medium heat. Once boiling, reduce the heat and simmer for 10 minutes. Remove from the heat and drain the carrots.

Place the carrots on a platter and top with the herbs, burrata, and garbanzo beans. Drizzle over the dressing and serve.

• •

store/make it vegan

You can pickle the carrots in advance—just let them cool completely and store in the refrigerator until ready to assemble the salad.

• •

This is inspired by a Shanghai poached chicken dish. If you don't have time to make the Asian oil, a quality store-bought one will do.

poached chicken salad
with scallions & rice

prep time: 5 minutes   **cook time:** 15 minutes   **serves:** 2

• •

2 skinless, boneless chicken breasts

1 lemongrass stalk, bashed

2-inch (5-cm) piece of ginger

½ bunch of scallions, finely chopped

1 garlic clove, minced

½ bunch of cilantro, chopped

1 tablespoon dark soy sauce

juice of 1 lime

4 tablespoons peanut oil

1 cucumber

1 handful of Thai basil leaves

1⅓ cups (250g) cooked jasmine rice
  (can be bought cooked in pouches)

2 tablespoons Asian-Infused Hot
  Crunchy Oil (page 203)

• •

Fill a medium saucepan with water, then add the chicken and bashed lemongrass and bring to a boil over medium heat. Once boiling, reduce the heat to a low simmer, cover with a lid, and poach the chicken for 10 minutes, or until the flesh is white and any juices run clear when a knife is inserted into the thickest part.

Meanwhile, grate the ginger into a heatproof bowl, then add the scallions, garlic, cilantro, soy sauce, and lime juice. Heat the oil in a small saucepan over high heat for a few minutes, then pour it over the ginger and let infuse.

Cut the cucumber in half, place on a cutting board, smash it with the back of a knife, then cut it on the bias. Add the cucumber to the ginger bowl with the basil and mix until combined.

Heat the rice until piping hot, then divide between two bowls. Top the rice with the cucumber. Remove the chicken from the pan with a spatula, cut into slices, and add to the bowls. Drizzle with the crunchy oil and serve at once.

• •

store/make it vegan

For a vegan option, use tempeh or silken tofu instead of the meat. Just drizzle it with soy sauce and sliced lemongrass instead.

143

• •

This warm, crunchy, creamy salad is a joy to eat in the fall. Use your favorite variety of blue cheese.

leek & blue cheese salad

with apple, celery & hazelnuts

prep time: 10 minutes   **cook time:** 8 minutes   **serves:** 2

• •

8 baby leeks, trimmed

1 red apple, sliced into matchsticks

2 celery stalks, sliced on the bias

1 large handful of mixed leaves

⅓ cup (50g) toasted hazelnuts

½ cup (60g) chopped blue cheese

4 tablespoons Dijon Dressing
   (page 187)

salt

• •

Bring a medium saucepan of water to a boil and season with salt. Add the leeks, reduce the heat, and simmer for 6 minutes. Using a slotted spoon or tongs, remove the leeks and let steam-dry.

Place a large stovetop grill pan over high heat and, when smoking hot, add the leeks, and char for 2 minutes on each side.

Remove the leeks from the pan, cut into slices, and add to a salad bowl along with all the remaining ingredients. Toss until everything is well combined, then serve.

• •

store
To make this vegan, omit the cheese and char some smoked tofu when cooking the leeks.
Swap the honey in the Dijon dressing for maple syrup.

145

• •

winter

seasonal veggies winter

leaves

chard

Chard, or Swiss chard, is sweeter than kale. It can be eaten as baby leaves or left to grow full size then wilted, much the same as spinach.

watercress

Watercress has a slightly bitter, peppery flavor and goes well with many vegetables that we associate with winter, such as carrots, beets, apples, and pears.

kale

In the winter, kale has thicker, curlier, and larger leaves, so is suited to heartier salads. Shredding it finely and then massaging it in oil with your hands for a few minutes makes it tender.

Tuscan kale

Tuscan kale, or cavolo nero, excels in winter salads. It has a sweeter and milder flavor than other kale, so pairs well with beets, leeks, and carrots.

cabbage

From red cabbage to savoy, cabbage is very useful in winter salads, either eaten raw or lightly cooked, such as the Charred Cabbage Salad on page 181.

roots

beets

Beets are best from spring until early winter. They have a sweet earthy taste that goes well with goat cheese, blue cheese, labneh, and other root vegetables.

baby potatoes

Winter baby potatoes have a delicate, sweet flavor and softer flesh than main potatoes, so are a delight to eat in warming salads in the depths of winter.

carrots

During winter, carrots develop a much sweeter taste, which pairs well with foods including beets, Brussels sprouts, potatoes, and leeks.

turnips

Turnips have a spicy, more pungent flavor and go well with other foods we associate with winter, including carrots, potatoes, sweet potatoes, and apples.

sweet potatoes

Sweet potatoes are one of the most versatile vegetables during late fall and winter. They pair well with carrots, ginger, citrus fruits, spinach, and mushrooms.

roots

kitchen garden

celery root

Celery root, or celeriac, is a root vegetable that's harvested in winter. It has a very distinctive taste—nutty and sweet with a strong celery flavor. It goes well with other root vegetables.

Jerusalem artichokes

Jerusalem artichokes are knobby tubers with a sweet, nutty, and earthy taste. They go well with other wintery foods, such as citrus fruit, spinach, and nuts.

purple sprouting broccoli

Purple sprouting broccoli, sometimes called winter sprouting broccoli, can cope with big flavors and is easily paired with peas, leeks, cabbage, and cheeses.

Brussels sprouts

Brussels sprouts are usually associated with winter, but they are available right through until March. They have a nutty flavor and go well with lime.

celery

Celery has a strong but mild flavor and makes a good addition to warming wintery salads alongside walnut, kale, cheese, leeks, and apples. Try the Manchego & Celery Salad on page 175.

fruit

pears

When completely ripe, pears become sweet and very juicy and so pair well with other winter foods, such as apples, cabbage, celery, squashes, cheese, and walnuts.

apples

There are so many apple varieties and flavors, from sweet and crunchy to tart, and they go well with other winter foods including pears, squash, kale, and warming spices.

winter citrus

All types of citrus fruit, including lemons and oranges, are at their best from winter through to March. They are very versatile and can be added to any dish to lift the flavor.

pomegranate

The sweet-tart flavor of pomegranate seeds pack a huge punch and go well with other winter fruits and vegetables, such as kale, cabbage, herbs, and citrus fruit.

dates

Medjool dates have a rich, caramel, and sweet flavor when ripe and are an excellent choice to add to winter fruit salads alongside oranges, clementines, apples, and walnuts.

If you have not tried farro before, here is a delicious introduction. The nutty farro and spicy pickled chiles work really well together here.

farro salad

with shredded Tuscan kale & pickled onions

prep time: 5 minutes **cook time:** 20 minutes **serves:** 2

• •

1 cup (200g) pearled farro

2 tablespoons olive oil, plus extra
  for drizzling

½ head of Tuscan kale, sliced

4 garlic cloves, sliced

zest and juice of 1 lemon

2 tablespoons Mexican-Infused
  Pickled Chiles, chopped (page 194)

scant ½ cup (50g) pecans, toasted
  and chopped

2 tablespoons Pickled Onions
  (page 195)

1 handful of parsley, chopped

¾ ounce (20g) Manchego cheese

salt and freshly ground black pepper

• •

Bring a medium saucepan of salted water to a rolling boil over high heat. Tip in the farro and boil for 15 to 20 minutes until the grain is al dente and a little chewy.

Meanwhile, heat a large skillet over high heat, add the olive oil, kale, and garlic, and fry for 3 minutes, or until the kale is vivid green and has wilted. Make sure you move it around so the garlic is evenly fried. Add the lemon zest and juice and fry for another minute. Season with salt and pepper and tip in the chopped pickled chiles. Remove the pan from the heat.

Once the farro is done, drain and tip it into the kale pan. Toss in the pecans, pickled onions, and chopped parsley, then divide between two plates.

Finish with an extra drizzle of olive oil and a grating of Manchego.

• •

store/make it vegan
If there is any salad leftover, let cool, then store in the refrigerator, and serve for lunch the following day.

• •

This fruit salad is so versatile. We uses blood oranges, but if they aren't available, then any winter fruit works brilliantly.

toasted oat citrus salad

with a thick yogurt & vanilla dressing

prep time: 5 minutes   **cook time:** 6 minutes   **serves:** 2

• •

1 cup (100g) rolled jumbo oats

½ cup (50g) chopped pecans

⅓ cup (50g) pumpkin seeds

1 tablespoon butter

2 tablespoons honey

2 blood oranges, peeled and sliced
  into circles, setting the zest
  of 1 orange aside

150g Greek thick yogurt

1 teaspoon vanilla bean paste

1 handful of mint leaves

• •

Heat a medium skillet over medium heat, add the oats, pecans, pumpkin seeds, and butter, and fry for 5 minutes, tossing constantly, or until golden and crisp. Add the honey and fry for another 1 minute, or until coated and sticky. Add the orange zest and toss through.

Mix the yogurt and vanilla together, then spoon into two bowls and top with the sliced orange. Finish with the toasted oat mixture and a sprinkling of mint. Serve at once.

• •

store/make it vegan
Make a double batch of the oat mixture, then store it in a clean jam jar for sprinkling over any winter fruit you like.

153

• •

This green noodle dish is perfect for when you need a speedy salad meal. Use any leafy greens you have and change them according to the season.

winter soba noodle salad

with miso & lime dressing

prep time: 10 minutes   **cook time:** 10 minutes   **serves:** 2

• •

7 ounces (200g) soba noodles

1 tablespoon peanut oil

3 garlic cloves, thinly sliced

2-inch (5-cm) piece of ginger,
  peeled and sliced into matchsticks

1 red chile, sliced

2 handfuls of Tuscan kale,
  thinly shredded

5 purple sprouting broccoli stalks,
  finely shredded

⅓ cup (50g) peanuts

1 jar Miso & Lime Dressing
  (page 188)

1 large handful of Thai basil,
  for garnish

• •

Bring a medium saucepan of water to a boil over high heat, add the noodles, and cook for 5 minutes, or until al dente. Drain and rinse under cold running water, then set the noodles aside.

Meanwhile, add the oil to a large skillet and place over high heat. Add the garlic, ginger, and chile and fry for 1 minute, tossing frequently. Add the kale and broccoli and fry for 4 minutes, mixing it around to make sure everything cooks evenly.

Add the noodles, peanuts, and dressing to the pan, toss to combine, then remove from the heat and divide between two plates. Garnish with Thai basil and serve.

• •

store/make it vegan
If you want to keep this, then store the cooked and rinsed noodles in a separate airtight container, tossing them together with the other ingredients before serving.

• •

This salad is packed with all those delicious, spicy flavors from the seeds and crunchy textures from the vegetables. Eat warm or cold.

kimchi noodle salad
with umami seeds

prep time: 10 minutes   **cook time:** 4 minutes   **serves:** 2

• •

7 ounces (200g) soba noodles

2-inch (5-cm) piece ginger,
   peeled and grated

2 garlic cloves, grated

1 tablespoon toasted sesame oil

1 tablespoon gochujang (chile paste)

juice of 1 lime

10½ ounces (300g) kimchi, chopped

1 carrot, julienned

3 scallions, sliced on the bias

1 handful of Brussels sprouts,
   finely sliced

3 tablespoons Umami Toasted Seeds
   (page 196)

1 handful of cilantro

• •

Bring a medium saucepan of water to a boil over high heat, add the noodles, and cook for 4 minutes, or until chewy and perfectly cooked.

Meanwhile, whisk the ginger, garlic, sesame oil, gochujang, and lime juice in a large bowl until smooth. Drain the noodles and tip into the bowl, then toss until the noodles are coated all over.

Add all the remaining ingredients to the noodles and give it a good mix to combine. Divide between two bowls and serve.

• •

store/make it vegan
You make this salad in advance and store it in the refrigerator to eat the following day.

• •

This salad comes together so quickly. It's flavorsome and packed with protein. Buy good-quality tuna in olive oil for maximum flavor.

lemon, kale & tuna salad

with egg & pecorino

prep time: 5 minutes   **cook time:** 7 minutes   **serves:** 2

· ·

½ lemon, chopped

7 ounces (200g) raw kale, shredded

3 eggs

1 small handful of shaved pecorino

¾ cup (100g) smoked almonds, sliced

7½ ounces (220g) jarred
  tuna, drained

3 tablespoons Dijon Dressing
  (page 187)

salt

· ·

Add the lemon and kale to a large bowl and season with salt. Using clean hands, give it all a good scrunch and set aside.

Have a bowl of ice water ready nearby. Bring a medium saucepan of water to a boil. Once boiling, gently add the eggs and simmer for 6½ minutes. Drain the eggs and add to the bowl of ice water. Once the eggs are cool enough to handle, peel and slice in half.

Toss all the ingredients together well, except for the eggs, in a large bowl. Top with the eggs and serve.

· ·

store/make it vegan

Prepare the kale and boil the eggs ahead of time, but peel the eggs just before serving.

This warm roast chicken is a joy of a salad. If you haven't tried a bitter leaf, they are at their best in winter.

roast chicken salad
with bitter leaves & a spicy lentil base

prep time: 5 minutes   **cook time:** 20 minutes   **serves:** 2

• •

1⅓ cups (250g) cooked Puy lentils
  (can be bought cooked in pouches)

1 red onion, cut into eighths

½ bunch of thyme

1 red chile, diced

5 garlic cloves, smashed

1 lemon, chopped

2 tablespoons olive oil

4 boneless chicken thighs, skin-on

2 heads of chicory, leaves separated

2 tablespoons Dijon Dressing
  (page 187)

salt and freshly ground black pepper

• •

Preheat the oven to 400°F (200°C).

Add the lentils, onion, thyme, chile, garlic, chopped lemon, and olive oil to a small baking dish, about 8 by 12 inches (20 by 30cm), and mix well until combined.

Top with the chicken and season generously with salt and pepper. Roast in the oven for 20 minutes, or until the juices run clear when a skewer is inserted into the thickest part of the meat.

When the chicken is cooked, remove the chicken from the dish and carve into slices. Toss the chicory through the lentils, then divide between two bowls. Top with the sliced chicken, and drizzle over the dressing.

• •

store/make it vegan

If you don't eat meat, this dish works well with roasted celery root. Just add and cook like you would chicken. Swap the honey in the dressing for maple syrup.

• •

This is a love letter to all winter root vegetables—packed full of flavor and is so delicious. If you are serving this platter as a feast, then add some charred flatbreads.

sharing platter

roast root veg salad on whipped feta

prep time: 20 minutes **cooking time:** 45 minutes **serves:** 6
..

1 celery root, 2 pounds 4 ounces (1kg), peeled and cut into 1½-inch (4-cm) chunks

8 Jerusalem artichokes, halved

1 onion squash, cut into thin boats

3 red onions, quartered

1 head of garlic, halved

juice of 2 lemons and 1 lemon, sliced

3 tablespoons olive oil

6-ounce (170-g) jar harissa paste

2 x 7-ounce (200-g) blocks of feta

scant 1 cup (200g) Greek yogurt

1 bunch of parsley, leaves picked

2 tablespoons za'atar

1 head of Tuscan kale

1 tablespoon cumin seeds

1 tablespoon sumac

1 handful of mint, parsley, and dill

¾ cup (100g) chopped almonds

3 tablespoons pomegranate molasses

salt

1. Preheat the oven to 400°F (200°C). Place the celery root, Jerusalem artichokes, squash, onion, garlic, and sliced lemon in a large roasting tray.

2. Toss through the olive oil, lemon juice, and harissa until well coated. Season generously with salt and roast in the oven for 30 minutes.

3. Meanwhile, add the feta, yogurt, and parsley to a blender and blend until smooth. Stir the za'atar through the feta mixture, then scoop out and set aside.

4. Remove the roasted vegetables from the oven and sprinkle the kale, cumin seeds, and sumac over the top. Roast for another 15 minutes, or until everything is cooked.

5. Spoon the feta mixture onto a large platter and spread it around, giving the vegetables a feta bed to sit on.

6. Top the feta mixture with all the roasted vegetables.

7. Sprinkle the herbs and chopped almonds over the vegetables, then drizzle the pomegranate molasses over the top.

8. Serve at once, letting guests help themselves.

This recipe has a lot of garlic but it works so well with the oily, lemony kale. I love this salad hot on those bitter wintery days.

garlic & pasta salad
with chile & Tuscan kale

prep time: 5 minutes **cook time:** 15 minutes **serves:** 2

• •

7 ounces (200g) orecchiette

scant ½ cup (100ml) olive oil

5 garlic cloves, sliced

1 teaspoon fennel seeds

1 red chile, sliced

1 head of Tuscan kale,
  finely chopped

zest and juice of ½ lemon

salt and freshly ground black pepper

¾ cup (50g) grated Parmesan,
  for serving

• •

Cook the orecchiette in a large saucepan of salted water for 8 to 10 minutes, or according to the package directions. Drain, setting 1 to 1¼ cups (250 to 300ml) of the cooking water aside.

Heat the olive oil in a large skillet over medium heat, add the garlic, fennel seeds, and chile, and fry for 2 minutes. Add the kale and fry for 3 minutes, or until just wilted and vivid green. Tip in the pasta and toss to combine.

Add the lemon zest and juice, then add a splash of the reserved pasta water and season with salt and pepper. Divide between two plates and serve with grated Parmesan.

• •

store/make it vegan
You can make this salad in advance and eat it cold.

• •

This poached fruit salad is a great way to use seasonal fruit. Serve with ice cream, on top of oatmeal, or even just as it is.

chamomile fruit salad

with mascarpone

prep time: 5 minutes **cook time:** 25 minutes **serves:** 2

• •

2 tablespoons honey

1 cup (250ml) white wine

1 tablespoon vanilla bean paste

juice of 1 lemon

2 apples, peeled and quartered

4 Medjool dates, pitted and chopped

2 clementines, peeled and segmented

2 chamomile tea bags

mascarpone or ice cream, for
    serving (optional)

• •

Bring the honey, white wine, vanilla, and lemon juice to a boil in a medium saucepan over medium heat. Once boiling, reduce the heat to a simmer and add the apples and dates. Simmer for 10 to 15 minutes, or until the apples are soft on the outside and hard on the inside.

Add the clementines and chamomile tea bags to the pan and remove from the heat. Let the fruit stand for 10 minutes.

When ready to eat, divide the fruit between two bowls and drizzle with the remaining liquid. Top with mascarpone or ice cream, if desired.

• •

store/make it vegan

After adding the clementines and chamomile tea bags to the apples, transfer to a bowl, cover, and let chill in the refrigerator overnight to serve the following day.

• •

A twist on the Hawaiian classic, the tuna is mixed with fresh ginger and kimchi to give it some heat. You can use sushi rice instead of brown rice.

winter poke bowl
with sweet potato & garlic greens

prep time: 10 minutes   **cook time:** 20 minutes   **serves:** 2

• •

1 sweet potato

4 tablespoons Miso & Lime Dressing
   (page 188)

7 ounces (200g) sushi-grade tuna

1¼-inch (3-cm) piece of ginger,
   peeled and grated

3½ ounces (100g) kimchi, chopped

1 tablespoon olive oil

2 garlic cloves, sliced

1 red chile, sliced

2 handfuls of Tuscan kale, chopped

1¾ cups (250g) cooked brown rice
   (can be bought cooked in pouches)

2 scallions, sliced on the bias

1 handful of mixed herbs

salt

• •

Preheat the oven to 350°F (180°C).

Cut the sweet potato into bite-size pieces, then spread the pieces out on a large baking sheet. Drizzle over 2 tablespoons of the dressing and mix well. Roast in the oven for 20 minutes, or until tender.

Meanwhile, cut the tuna into ¾-inch (2-cm) chunks, then mix the tuna, grated ginger, and kimchi together in a large bowl until everything is well combined. Season with a little salt and let chill in the refrigerator.

Place a large skillet over medium heat, add the olive oil, then add the garlic and chile and fry for 4 to 5 minutes. Add the kale and fry for 3 minutes, or until wilted. Remove the pan from the heat.

Heat the rice until piping hot, then divide it between two bowls. Top with equal amounts of greens, roasted sweet potato, and tuna. Sprinkle with scallions and herbs, then drizzle over the remaining dressing and serve at once.

• •

store/make it vegan
For a vegan option replace the tuna with tofu. Pan-fry the tofu and ginger until crispy, then mix it with the kimchi.

• •

This sweet, salty raw salad is full of flavor. The kale gives you that nourishing kick your body needs in the dark months.

Manchego & celery salad

with smoked almonds & a herb dressing

prep time: 5 minutes   **cook time:** 0 minutes   **serves:** 2

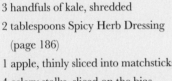

3 handfuls of kale, shredded

2 tablespoons Spicy Herb Dressing
  (page 186)

1 apple, thinly sliced into matchsticks

4 celery stalks, sliced on the bias

scant ½ cup (60g) roasted smoked
  almonds, chopped

4 Medjool dates, pitted and chopped

1¾ ounces (50g) Manchego
  cheese, shaved

Add the kale to a large bowl and pour in the dressing. Using clean hands, give the kale a good scrunch.

Toss through all the remaining ingredients, finishing with the cheese. Serve at once.

store/make it vegan
To make this vegan, leave out the cheese and sprinkle with toasted pumpkin seeds.

This salad takes some chopping but then comes together so quickly. If you have a jar of Crispy Onions (page 197), it's a great add on.

Thai-inspired raw salad
with Thai chile & ginger dressing

prep time: 10 minutes   **cook time:** 0 minutes   **serves:** 2

2 turnips, peeled and julienned

1 carrot, julienned

½ white cabbage, shredded

5½ ounces (150g) cooked shrimp

1 large handful of Thai basil

1 large handful of cilantro

1 handful of Umami Toasted Seeds (page 196)

4 tablespoons of Thai Chile & Ginger Dressing (page 189)

Crispy Onion (page 197), for topping (optional)

Place the turnips, carrot, cabbage, shrimp, herbs, and toasted seeds in a large bowl and add the dressing. Toss until all the ingredients are well mixed and coated in the dressing, then divide between two plates. Top with the crispy onions, if using, and serve.

store/make it vegan

For a vegan option, omit the shrimp and use pan-fried tofu instead.

salad in a jar

This salad is super easy to pull together—just toss it all together and serve. It works well for a packed lunch or post-gym dinner.

raw rainbow chop salad
with almonds, herbs & pickled onions

prep time: 10 minutes   **cook time:** 0 minutes   **serves:** 2

• •

2 handfuls of kale, thinly shredded

4 tablespoons Citrus Dressing
(page 190)

1⅓ cups (250g) cooked Puy lentils
(can be bought cooked in pouches)

1 yellow or orange beet, thinly sliced

1 pear, sliced

3 celery stalks, sliced on the bias

scant ½ cup (50g) pecans, toasted
and chopped

3½ ounces (100g) soft goat cheese
or feta

4 tablespoons Umami Toasted Seeds
(page 196)

salt and freshly ground black pepper

• •

Add the kale to a large bowl, then add 1 tablespoon of the dressing and, using clean hands, give the kale a good scrunch for 2 minutes. Season with salt and pepper.

Divide the lentils between two 17-ounce (500-ml) mason jars and divide the kale between them. Top with the sliced beet, pear, celery, pecans, goat cheese, and toasted seeds, then pour the remaining dressing equally between the jars.

• •

store/make it vegan
Put the other jar in the refrigerator and eat the following day.

177

• •

We use a shortcut in this dish by adding a store-bought tikka paste. You can use any Indian curry store-bought pastes you like.

Indian spice potato salad

with crispy naan toppers & mango dressing

prep time: 5 minutes   **cook time:** 35 minutes   **serves:** 2

• •

9 ounces (250g) baby
   potatoes, halved

2 tablespoons tikka paste

1 tablespoon cumin seeds

1 naan bread, torn into
   bite-size chunks

2 tablespoons coconut oil

1 carrot, peeled into long strips

1 handful of spinach leaves

⅓ cup (50g) cashew nuts, toasted

2 tablespoons mango chutney

zest and juice of 1 lime

1 bunch of cilantro, chopped

1 red chile, sliced

• •

Preheat the oven to 350°F (180°C).

Bring the potatoes to a boil in a medium saucepan of water. Boil for 15 minutes, or until tender, then drain and spread out on a large baking sheet. Add the tikka paste and cumin seeds, and toss until everything is combined. Add the coconut oil then roast in the oven for 10 minutes. Remove from the oven, add the torn naan, then bake for another 10 minutes, or until the naan is crispy.

Add the carrot, spinach, and cashews to a large a serving bowl.

Mix the mango chutney, lime juice, and 2 tablespoons water in a small bowl to a dressing consistency. Add the potatoes to the salad bowl, then add the dressing and toss together until combined. Finish with grated lime zest, chopped cilantro, and sliced chile.

• •

store/make it vegan

If storing, keep the potatoes and naan separate and toss in the dressing before serving.

• •

If you've never tried freekeh, this recipe is a great place to start. Cooking the cabbage on a stovetop grill pan makes a winter meal.

charred cabbage salad
with freekeh & tahini dressing

prep time: 10 minutes   **cook time:** 20 minutes   **serves:** 2

• •

scant ⅔ cup (100g) freekeh

1 lemon, halved

1 conehead or green
   cabbage, quartered

3 tablespoons harissa paste

1 handful of pomegranate seeds

1 handful of mint leaves

1 handful of parsley

1 handful of dill

scant 1 cup (100g) toasted pistachios,
   coarsely chopped

3 tablespoons Tahini & Miso
   Dressing (page 187)

salt and freshly ground black pepper

• •

Rinse the freekeh under cold running water, then tip it into a medium saucepan and toast for a few minutes over high heat. Fill the pan with boiling water and bring to a boil. Add the lemon halves, then reduce the heat to a simmer, cover with a lid, and cook for 20 minutes, or until the freekeh is tender. Once cooked, drain, removing the lemon halves and setting them aside.

Meanwhile, heat a stovetop grill pan over high heat. Cover the cabbage in the harissa paste, rubbing it all over. Once the pan is smoking hot, add the cabbage and char for a few minutes on each side.

Chop half of the cooked lemon, skin and all. (After roasting, the lemon peel becomes much softer and less bitter.) Add it to a large bowl with the pomegranate seeds, mint, parsley, dill, and pistachios. Season with salt and pepper.

Add the freekeh to the herb bowl with most of the dressing. Toss, then divide between two plates and top with the charred cabbage. Drizzle over the remaining dressing.

• •

store
To store, toss it all together, except for the dressing, in an airtight container and keep it in the refrigerator. Add the dressing just before serving.

• •

This dish is brilliant eaten either warm or cold, and is also good served with broiled shrimp, if you want to make a feast of it.

winter green pesto salad

with Israeli couscous

prep time: 10 minutes   **cook time:** 10 minutes   **serves:** 2

• •

1 cup (200g) Israeli couscous

6 tablespoons olive oil, divided

1 head broccoli, cut into tiny florets

2 handfuls of Swiss chard,
   finely chopped

4 garlic cloves, chopped

1 bunch of basil

¾ cup (100g) toasted cashew nuts

2 tablespoons nutritional yeast

¾ cup (50g) grated Parmesan

zest and juice of 1 lemon

2 tablespoons Pickled Onions
   (page 195)

2 tablespoons Pangrattato Crumb
   (page 201)

salt

• •

Bring a large saucepan of salted water to a boil. Once boiling, add the couscous and cook for 6 to 8 minutes, or according to the package directions. Drain and set aside in a large bowl.

Meanwhile, heat 3 tablespoons of the olive oil in a large skillet over high heat, add the broccoli, and fry for 5 minutes. Add the chard and garlic and fry for another 5 minutes, or until the chard is a soft green color.

Add the basil, cashews, nutritional yeast, Parmesan, and lemon zest and juice to a food processor. Pour over the remaining oil and 2 tablespoons water and blend until smooth.

Add the green sauce to the couscous and mix until well combined. Divide between two plates and top with the pickled onions and the crumb.

• •

store/make it vegan

For a vegan option, omit the Parmesan. You can add extra cashews, if desired.

• •

dressings,
pickles, toppers
& oils

dressings

Parmesan dressing

1 garlic clove, peeled
6 good-quality canned anchovies
  in olive oil
1½ cups (300g) Greek yogurt
zest and juice of 1 lemon

¾ cup (50g) grated Parmesan
2 tablespoons olive oil
1 teaspoon Dijon mustard
salt (optional)

Blitz all the ingredients in a food processor until smooth. Taste and add a little salt, if needed. Store in the refrigerator for a few days.
prep time: 5 minutes **makes:** 8-ounce (250-ml) jar

spicy herb dressing

1 bunch of cilantro
10 pickled jalapeño chiles
1 garlic clove, peeled
juice of 1 lime
⅔ cup (150ml) olive oil

½ teaspoon ground cumin
1 red chile, diced
1 teaspoon maple syrup
salt and freshly ground
  black pepper

Blitz all the ingredients in a food processor until it is a vivid green dressing. Taste, season, and blitz one more time. Store in the refrigerator for a few days.
prep time: 5 minutes **makes:** 8-ounce (250-ml) jar

Dijon dressing

1 garlic clove, grated
1 teaspoon honey
1 tablespoon Dijon mustard
1 teaspoon red wine vinegar

6 tablespoons olive oil
½ teaspoon salt

Add all the ingredients to a clean jam jar, close with the lid, and give it a really good shake until smooth and glossy. Store in the refrigerator and shake before using. It will keep in the refrigerator for a week.
prep time: 5 minutes   **makes:** 8-ounce (250-ml) jar

tahini & miso dressing

1 tablespoon miso paste
1 teaspoon maple syrup
2 tablespoons tahini

zest and juice of 1 lime
2 tablespoons peanut oil

Add all the ingredients with 2 tablespoons water to a clean jam jar, close with the lid, and shake vigorously until thick and glossy. Taste and add a little extra water, if needed. Store in the refrigerator for a week.
prep time: 5 minutes   **makes:** 8-ounce (250-ml) jar

187

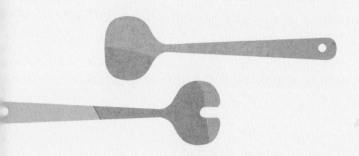

green goddess jalapeño dressing

1 large handful of parsley & stems
6 jalapeño chiles
1 large handful of basil
1 large handful of chives
½ cup (60g) cashew nuts

2 garlic cloves
zest and juice of 1 lemon
1 tablespoon nutritional yeast
8 tablespoons olive oil
½ teaspoon salt

Blend all the ingredients in a small blender until smooth. Store in the refrigerator for one to two days.

prep time: 5 minutes   **makes:** 8-ounce (250-ml) jar

miso & lime dressing

2-inch (5-cm) piece of ginger,
  peeled and grated
2 garlic cloves, grated
2 shallots, chopped
4 tablespoons toasted sesame oil

2 tablespoons rice wine vinegar
2 teaspoons brown miso paste
1 red chile, diced
zest and juice of 2 limes

Mix all the ingredients in a bowl until the miso is evenly incorporated. Store in the refrigerator for a week.

prep time: 5 minutes   **makes:** 8-ounce (250-ml) jar

Thai chile & ginger dressing

2 garlic cloves
6 red Thai chiles
2-inch (5-cm) piece of ginger,
  peeled and grated
juice of 2 limes

1 teaspoon soft brown sugar
2½ tablespoons fish sauce
3 tablespoons peanut oil

Add the garlic and chiles to a mortar and pestle and bash until broken
down. Add the ginger, lime juice, sugar, fish sauce, and oil and mix until
all the sugar has broken down. Store in the refrigerator for three days.
prep time: 5 minutes   **makes:** 8-ounce (250-ml) jar

za'atar dressing

4 teaspoons za'atar
juice of 1 lemon
1 garlic clove, grated
5 tablespoons olive oil

½ teaspoon salt
2 teaspoons sumac

Add all the ingredients to a clean jam jar, close with the lid, and shake
until smooth. Store in the refrigerator for a week.
prep time: 5 minutes   **makes:** 8-ounce (250-ml) jar

herby dressing

½ bunch of cilantro
½ bunch of parsley
½ bunch of dill
2 tablespoons capers
1 tablespoon red wine vinegar

1 garlic clove
8 tablespoons olive oil
1 red chile, diced
Salt and freshly ground
    black pepper

Chop all the herbs and add to a bowl. Coarsely chop the capers and add to the bowl with all the remaining ingredients. Mix together. Taste and adjust the seasoning, if needed. Store in the refrigerator for two days.
prep time: 5 minutes   **makes:** 8-ounce (250-ml) jar

citrus dressing

juice of 2 lemons
juice of 2 limes
6 tablespoons olive oil
2 teaspoons runny honey
Salt

Add all the ingredients to a clean jar, season with salt, close with a lid, and shake well until it is emulsified. Store in the refrigerator for a week.
prep time: 5 minutes   **makes:** 8-ounce (250-ml) jar

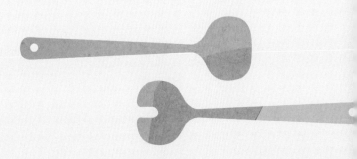

peanut & sesame dressing

2-inch (5-cm) piece of ginger
1 garlic clove
1 tablespoon smooth peanut butter
1 tablespoon tahini

1 teaspoon toasted sesame oil
1 teaspoon maple syrup
1 teaspoon rice vinegar
1 tablespoon light soy sauce

Coarsely chop the ginger and garlic and add it to a small blender with all the remaining ingredients. Blend until smooth. Store in the refrigerator for a week.
prep time: 5 minutes   **makes:** 8-ounce (250-ml) jar

chile dressing

4 tablespoons store-bought crunchy chile oil
2 tablespoons soy sauce
4 tablespoons toasted sesame oil
2 tablespoons rice vinegar

Whisk all the ingredients together in a small bowl until combined, then store in a jar. It will keep in the refrigerator for a week.
prep time: 5 minutes   **makes:** 8-ounce (250-ml) jar

pickles

rhubarb & carrot pickle

4 rhubarb stalks
3 baby carrots, peeled
scant 1 cup (200ml) cider vinegar
1 teaspoon sea salt

2 tablespoons superfine sugar
½ teaspoon hot pepper flakes
1 tablespoon yellow mustard seed
1 teaspoon fennel seeds

Cut the rhubarb into equal 1½-inch (3-cm) lengths. Quarter the carrots. Place the remaining ingredients with ⅔ cup (150ml) water into a medium cast-iron pan and gently simmer until the sugar has dissolved. Cool completely. Pack the rhubarb and carrots into a sterilized mason jar and pour over the cooled liquid. Seal and keep in a cool, dark place for a week and up to two months. Once open, chill. Eat within two weeks.
prep time: 10 minutes   **cook time:** 5 minutes   **makes:** 1¾ cups (400ml)

sweet & sour cucumber pickle

1 pound (450g) cucumbers	2 tablespoons sea salt
3 long green chiles	1 tablespoon coriander seeds
¾ ounce (20g) dill	1 teaspoon peppercorns
¼ cup (60ml) white wine vinegar	1 teaspoon mustard seeds

Wash the cucumbers, chiles, and dill. Make the brine by mixing 1½ cups (350ml) water, vinegar, and salt. Pack the cucumbers and chiles into a jar, coarsely chop the dill, and add to the jar with the coriander seeds, peppercorns, and mustard seeds. Fill the jar with the brine, making sure the cucumbers are fully submerged. Seal the jar and let pickle in the refrigerator for at least 48 hours. Once opened, eat within two months.
prep time: 10 minutes   **cook time:** 0 minutes   **makes:** 1¾ cups (400ml)

Mexican-infused pickled chiles

1¾ cups (400ml) white
  wine vinegar
1 cup (200g) superfine sugar

1 tablespoon coriander seeds
20 jalapeño chiles, sliced

Bring the vinegar, 1¼ cups (300ml) water, sugar, and coriander seeds to a gentle boil
in a saucepan. Add the jalapeños and mix to combine. Pour into a sterilized jar and,
once cool, store, unopened, in the refrigerator for up to two months. Once opened, eat
within two months.
prep time: 5 minutes   **cook time:** 5 minutes   **makes:** 1¾ cups (400ml)

pickled onions

scant ½ cup (100ml) white
wine vinegar
juice of 1 lemon

1 tablespoon superfine sugar
1 teaspoon salt
4 red onions, thinly sliced

Heat the vinegar and lemon juice in a saucepan over medium heat for
2 minutes. Add all the remaining ingredients to the pan and, using clean hands, give the
onions a good scrunch. Press into a sterilized jar, pour over any remaining liquid, and
keep in the refrigerator. Use these immediately. Once opened, eat within two months.
prep time: 5 minutes   **cook time:** 2 minutes   **makes:** 34-ounce (1-litre) jar

195

toppings

umami toasted seeds

generous 2 cups (300g) mixed
  seeds—we used pumpkin,
  sunflower, and sesame seeds

2 tablespoons tamari
1 teaspoon maple syrup

Toast all the seeds to a large skillet over medium heat until the seeds are popping and
cracking. Remove from the heat, add the tamari and maple syrup, and mix thoroughly.
Let cool, then spoon into a sterilized jar. Keep in a cool, dark place for up to a month.
prep time: 5 minutes **cook time:** 6 minutes **makes:** 8-ounce (250-ml) jar

crispy onions

1¾ cups (400ml) light oil, such as
vegetable oil
20 shallots, thinly sliced
1 teaspoon flaky sea salt

Line a baking sheet with paper towels. Heat the oil in a large, heavy-bottomed skillet
over medium heat, add the shallots, and fry for 20 minutes, or until golden brown,
making sure to move the onions around the pan frequently so they get an even coloring.
Using a large slotted spoon, scoop the onions onto the lined sheet tray and let cool
completely. Spoon into a medium jar. Keep in a cool, dark place for up to a month.
prep time: 15 minutes   **cook time:** 20 minutes   **makes:** 8-ounce (250-ml) jar

197

● ●

crispy garbanzo beans

14-ounce (400-g) can garbanzo
  beans, drained and rinsed
1 teaspoon kosher salt
3 tablespoons olive oil

zest of 1 lemon
1 teaspoon hot pepper flakes

Preheat the oven to 425°F (220°C). Pat the garbanzos dry on a clean dish towel. Tip
them into a bowl, add the salt and oil, and toss until coated. Spread them evenly onto
a baking sheet and roast for 15 minutes. Add the lemon zest and pepper and roast until
golden and crisp. Cool. Store in a clean jar for a week.
prep time: 5 minutes   **cook time:** 30 minutes   **makes:** 8-ounce (250-ml) jar

rye-baked croutons

4 slices rye sourdough bread, cut
into 2-inch (5-cm) chunks
½ cup (120ml) light olive oil
½ teaspoon kosher salt

freshly ground black pepper
2 large garlic cloves, minced

Preheat the oven to 375°F (190°C). Toss the bread with the oil until evenly saturated.
Season generously with the salt and pepper. Arrange in a single layer on a large baking
sheet and bake for 10 minutes. Remove, add the garlic, and toss through. Bake for
another 10 minutes until crisp. Let cool, then keep in a clean jar for up to a week.
prep time: 5 minutes   **cook time:** 20 minutes   **makes:** 14-ounce (400-ml) jar

jar croutons

10½ ounces (300g) sourdough
  bread, cut into cubes
3 tablespoons olive oil

2 teaspoons red wine vinegar
salt

Preheat the oven to 350°F (180°C). Line a baking sheet with baking parchment. Place
the bread in a large bowl, add the olive oil, vinegar, and salt and toss until the bread
is coated. Spread over the lined baking sheet in a single layer and bake for 15 to 20
minutes, tossing halfway through. Let cool. Keep in an airtight jar for two weeks.
prep time: 5 minutes **cook time:** 20 minutes **makes:** 17-ounce (500-ml) jar

pangrattato crumb

10½ ounces (300g) sourdough or
stale bread
3½ tablespoons olive oil

1 garlic clove, grated
zest of 1 lemon
1 teaspoon fennel seeds
large pinch of hot pepper flakes

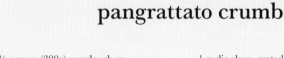

Blitz the bread in a food processor to coarse crumbs. Heat the oil in a large skillet over medium heat, add the breadcrumbs, and fry for 5 minutes. Add the garlic and lemon zest and fry until golden and crisp, tossing frequently. Add the fennel seeds and hot pepper flakes and toast for 1 minute. Cool. Use at once or store in a jar for a few days.
prep time: 5 minutes   **cook time:** 20 minutes   **makes:** 10-ounce (300-ml) jar

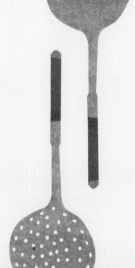

oils

chile-infused oil

generous 2 cups (500ml) extra-
   virgin olive oil
10 dried red chiles
2 rosemary sprigs

Add all the ingredients to a clean glass 25-ounce (750-ml) bottle. The
longer you leave this, the spicier it will become.
prep time: 5 minutes **cook time:** 0 minutes **makes:** generous 2 cups (500ml)

woody herb oil

1 bunch of woody herbs, such as
   rosemary, thyme, and oregano
1¾ cups (400ml) olive oil

Heat the herbs and oil in a small pan over medium heat for 5 minutes.
Remove from heat and set aside. Transfer to an airtight container and let
infuse for 8 to 12 hours. Strain the oil through cheesecloth, discarding the
herbs. Pour into a glass 25-ounce (750-ml) bottle. Use when needed.
prep time: 5 minutes **cook time:** 5 minutes **makes:** 1¾ cups (400ml)

citrus skin oil

3 lemons
4 garlic cloves, smashed
1¾ cups (400ml) olive oil

Using a vegetable peeler, peel the skins of the lemons into a medium saucepan. Place over medium heat and add the garlic. Toast for a few minutes, then pour in the oil and let stand for a few hours. Pour the oil into a 25-ounce (750-ml) bottle and add five strands of peel and the garlic.
prep time: 10 minutes   **cook time:** 5 minutes   **makes:** 1¾ cups (400ml)

Asian-infused hot crunchy oil

8 shallots, sliced
1¾ cups (400ml) peanut oil
5 to 6 garlic cloves, finely sliced
2½ ounces (75g) dried red chiles
2½ ounces (70g) hot pepper flakes

¼ cup (40g) superfine sugar
generous ¼ cup (70ml) soy sauce
1 star anise
3 tablespoons peanuts, chopped

Line a plate with paper towels. Cook the shallots in the oil for 15 minutes. Add the garlic and cook until crispy. Put the shallots and garlic onto the plate. Add the remaining ingredients to a 17-ounce (500-ml) jar. Add the oil. Stir, then add the shallots and garlic. Cool, then steep for two days.
prep time: 10 minutes   **cook time:** 18 minutes   **makes:** 1¾ cups (400ml)

• •

index

..

..

• •

Emily Ezekiel

acknowledgments

London born and bred, Emily currently works as a food author, art director, and food and prop stylist in the heart of Hackney, East London. She has worked in the food industry for over 15 years and during this period, she has gathered a wealth of experience across an impressive portfolio of food-related, creative projects and clients. She has worked alongside the most well-respected and best-loved names in the industry, some of these include Jamie Oliver, Nigella Lawson, and Anna Jones.

This book only comes together because it has a brilliant team behind it. Firstly, I'd like to thank Catie Ziller and Hardie Grant North America for once again trusting me with this privilege—I love writing books so it's a true honor.

My work wife, incredible friend, and continuous creative partner Issy Croker, for being the best food photographer going. Without you this book would be a lot less beautiful, and the shoot would have been much less fun. Thank you for always having my back and being by my side in our careers. I can't wait to see what the future brings for us both.

Joseph Denison Carey for being my right-hand man, for cooking and testing most of the recipes, playing some incredible playlists to keep us going through the long shoot days, and always being the brilliant, hilarious ray of light we need.

My husband Sebastian and best friend Athina for keeping me sane while writing and testing this book. Really I owe it all to you both.

To my editor Kathy for being so utterly brilliant with my words and making it all make sense and pointing out any missing edits. Thank you for all your help always. The designer Alice, for laying this book out and making it all look so lovely. Finally, thank you to all the interns who came and helped us with the piles of dishes, dashes to the shops, and general brilliance. Thank you Sophie, Franzi, Rosie, and anyone else I've missed.

Hardie Grant North America
2912 Telegraph Ave
Berkeley, CA 94705
hardiegrantusa.com

Text © 2023 by Emily Ezekiel
Photographs © 2023 by Issy Croker
Illustrations © 2023 by Alice Chadwick

Published in the United States by Hardie Grant North America, an imprint of Hardie Grant Publishing Pty Ltd.
Library of Congress Cataloging-in-Publication Data is available upon request
ISBN: 9781958417478
eBook ISBN: 9781958417485

Acquiring Editor: Catie Ziller
Photographer: Issy Croker
Food & prop stylist: Emily Ezekiel
Designer & illustrator: Alice Chadwick
Copy Editor: Kathy Steer

Printed in China

FIRST EDITION

Hardie Grant
PUBLISHING

FSC
www.fsc.org
MIX
Paper | Supporting responsible forestry
FSC® C020056